Career Diaries

Through the Eyes of a Funeral Director

True stories about life as a funeral
director including the good, the
bad, the funny & the unusual

LYNDA CHELDELIN FELL

with

BRIAN M. VAN HECK

FOREWORD BY
BRIAN M. VAN HECK

AlyBlue
MEDIA

Career Diaries
Through the Eyes of a Funeral Director– 1st ed.
True stories about life as a funeral director including the good,
the bad, the funny & the unusual
Lynda Cheldelin Fell/Brian M. Van Heck
Grief Diaries www.GriefDiaries.com

Cover Design by AlyBlue Media, LLC
Interior Design by AlyBlue Media LLC
Published by AlyBlue Media, LLC

ISBN: 978-1-944328-43-6
Library of Congress Control Number: 2017952651
AlyBlue Media, LLC
Ferndale, WA 98248
www.AlyBlueMedia.com

This book is designed to provide informative narrations to readers. It is sold with the understanding that the writers, authors or publisher is not engaged to render any type of psychological, legal, or any other kind of professional advice. The content is the sole expression and opinion of the authors and writers. No warranties or guarantees are expressed or implied by the choice to include any of the content in this book. Neither the publisher nor the author or writers shall be liable for any physical, psychological, emotional, financial, or commercial damages including but not limited to special, incidental, consequential or other damages. Our views and rights are the same: You are responsible for your own choices, actions and results.

PRINTED IN THE UNITED STATES OF AMERICA

THROUGH THE EYES OF A FUNERAL DIRECTOR

DEDICATION

This book is dedicated to funeral directors
everywhere. Thank you for your service.

CONTENTS

BY BRIAN VAN HECK

FOREWORD

And the Master had his hands in it.....

How does a project such as authoring a book come to fruition? Throughout my almost twenty year career in funeral service I have made the comment, "That's another chapter for my book," dozens of times. Those remarks were always tongue and cheek with the thought that someday it would be nice to write a book about the journey I embarked on. So as I pen the words of this introduction, it is with great pride but also great humility that a dream is coming true. The story of how this project came to be is one that is full of grief and heartache, but also of hope and faith. It was clearly orchestrated by someone greater than us funeral directors who answered life's calling.

One spring morning as I sat in my office preparing for the day ahead, I received a phone call from a young woman who needed to interview a funeral director to fulfill a requirement for a class she was taking at the local university. I had vowed to myself that if I ever was in a leadership role anytime a student approached me about the funeral profession, I would give them whatever I could. I made this vow because there were several funeral directors who gave me time when I was a student.

Emily, like most good college students, called me on a Wednesday for a paper due on Friday. I agreed to meet her at the funeral home the next day, Thursday. Little did I know that my willingness to give back to this student would lead to an entire book about the world of funeral directors.

When I met with Emily, I soon discovered that she was in the midst of her own grief since losing her roommate to suicide. She was not a procrastinating college student after all; she was just being real, authentic and raw. She didn't want to come to the funeral home for fear of her own emotional response—a reaction us funeral directors face each day. Each time we greet a family at the door, we meet individuals who don't want to be there, afraid of what their emotional response might be, and who know nothing about what to expect.

I did my best to answer Emily's questions that morning. As time went on, she shared more of her story and how she had found healing in her grief by writing her story in two books of the Grief Diaries series. She went on to tell me all about the series and gave me copies of the two books she had contributed to. Additionally, she told me that Lynda Cheldelin Fell was looking to create a book for funeral directors and asked if I was interested in participating. A few days later Lynda and I were conversing and sharing ideas on how to bring this book to fruition.

As our conversation progressed, it quickly became more than just completing an assignment for Emily; she was genuinely intrigued by funeral service and the role of funeral directors. Despite living in a death denying society, there is a unique fascination and curiosity around death. This is evident anytime I'm in a new social setting and I'm asked that infamous question, "What do you do?" Invariably, a litany of questions and intrigue follows.

Whatever your reason for picking up this book, it is my hope that you will be intrigued, inspired, and blessed by the journeys that my fellow funeral directors and I travel each day, when we walk with grieving families.

To God be the glory,

Brian M. Van Heck
Funeral Director
bmvanheck@msn.com

BY LYNDA CHELDELIN FELL

Preface

One night in 2007, I had a vivid dream. I was the front passenger in a car and my teen daughter Aly was sitting behind the driver. Suddenly the car missed a curve in the road and sailed into a lake. The driver and I escaped the sinking car, but Aly did not. As I bobbed to the surface, I dove again and again in the murky water desperately searching for my daughter. But I failed to find her. She was gone. My beloved daughter was gone, leaving nothing but an open book floating on the water where she disappeared.

Two years later, on August 5, 2009, that horrible nightmare became reality when Aly died as a backseat passenger in a car accident. Returning home from a swim meet, the car carrying Aly was T-boned by a father coming home from work. My beautiful fifteen-year-old daughter took the brunt of the impact and died instantly. She was the only fatality.

Within forty-eight hours I found myself in a funeral home tasked with making arrangements to lay our daughter to rest. With autopilot and adrenaline at the helm, I remember very little of this time.

In the eight years since I've often reflected back and wondered how the funeral staff dealt with bereaved mothers like me. When we come through the door, do they cringe? Do they draw straws or feign sudden illness and leave us in the hands of a less savvy coworker? No. Of course not, because the funeral industry is a calling that only the finest humanitarians answer. The funeral industry is a different sort of business, and it takes a special sort of person to work there.

Funeral directors and embalmers are college-educated men and women who purposely choose a career based around caregiving. They sacrifice sleep and precious family time to ensure that our need for loving guidance in our darkest hour is met, because death doesn't always happen during banking hours. By laying loved ones to rest, they offer the living the first steps toward healing. And they do it all without accolades.

If the funeral industry is based around caregiving, then why does a funeral cost so much? Because funeral homes have codes to follow, equipment to maintain, staff to pay, and student loans to pay off. When you eat in a restaurant, you pay for the food and the chef who prepared it. When you hire a doctor to bring your baby safely into this world, you pay for their service. When you hire a funeral home to help your family memorialize their loved one, it is no different. They are there around the clock to ensure your every wish is lovingly granted with kid gloves.

Death is an inevitable part of life nobody gets to skip. But when you too find yourself leaning on a funeral director in your darkest hour, it is comforting to know that he or she chose this career as a calling. One they wouldn't change for the world.

Warm regards,

Lynda Cheldelin Fell
CREATOR, REAL LIFE DIARIES

CHAPTER ONE

The Inspiration

It matters not what someone is born, but
what they grow to be. -J.K. ROWLING

Some children want to be an astronaut when they grow up. Others want to be a scientist or professional athlete. Very few set their sights on becoming one of the oldest professions in the world: a funeral director. A unique career, some are born into a family of undertakers. Others are drawn in by the interesting aspects. All are dedicated to serving societal needs to lay our loved ones to rest. How did you become involved in the funeral industry?

*

STEPHEN BARON
Stephen is a 64-year-old funeral service
licensee in Grand Haven, Michigan

I was born into a funeral service family. The youngest of three children, I do not remember a time when funeral service was not a topic of conversation. Funeral service did not exist within our home, but rather our home existed within funeral service. I was brought up the way many funeral directors' children were trained for decades: to argue with siblings in a whisper, to eat many meals that were made up of cold-cuts and salads as to not fill the building with smells of cooking food, to spend little time talking on the phone with friends, to watch television with no sound and to be aware that father's business was in reality that of the whole family. How we behaved was a reflection on "the business." It was little wonder that many of my close childhood friends were children of the local clergy. I later came to realize how closely related the two "callings" are.

Growing up, I was always intrigued with my father's work, but like most people, so much of it I did not understand. As I grew older, although I was not aware of it, I was learning many skills by watching him interact with both families and friends. It was no wonder that by the age of six, I was conducting funerals for wild birds and pets with my friend, the clergy's son.

It became increasingly impossible for my father to keep me from showing up at the breakfast table wearing a tie in hopes that I would be given a work assignment. Often I was given errands in keeping with my age and ability. I moved from taking obituary copy to the local paper, to washing cars and mowing the lawn, to assisting in lining up funeral processions, and finally riding along on first calls and ambulance runs in order to experience what was to lie ahead. My older brother would refer to my strong desire to follow Dad around as, "running for the office of town undertaker." He had already crossed the threshold and moved far beyond the idea of participating in Dad's work, except for the occasional setting of the chapel for a service. That day would come for me too. I discovered that there were other interests that were worth my attention: cars, girls and rock 'n' roll to start the list. That, and having a reliable paying job to enable my enjoyment of the aforementioned three.

Traveling down the road of being a teenager has its rewards and its pitfalls and disappointments, but none can compare to the news I came home to on a warm spring day during my sixteenth year. My father had been feeling tired for some time and because of this went to see his friend who was also his doctor. He had undergone the usual series of medical tests, one thing led to another and on that particular day he was given the diagnosis of multiple myeloma, a cancer of plasma cells. He was fifty-six years of age and was given two to five years to live. He lived eighteen months. He was fifty-eight, I was eighteen.

His death would mark a major turning point in my life. It was the marker for most of my decisions, good and bad, that I made for the next several years. His death, in large part, defined who and what I was to become.

My father had made one of the tougher changes in his career less than three years before learning of his illness. After thirty-three years, he left his sole proprietorship business in a small town and joined what was one of the largest firms in the region's largest city. A long established, multi-generational firm that was privileged to serve the families of many of the area's captains of business and industry, and many of the families who dedicated the talents and skills to those businesses. It was then, and remains, one of the area's most prestigious firms serving the area's diverse and growing population with pride. It has been a great honor to be associated with the many professionals, their reputations and legacies, past and present, that have been associated with this firm over the last 120 years and more.

Throughout the visitation hours, prior to Dad's funeral service, I heard from people about their experiences surrounding deaths within their families and how my father helped them in various ways to "move forward" from their loss. It was because of those stories that the seed that had been planted within me as a young boy began to grow. I clearly remember recognizing that my father was "called" to his profession and that his main objective was to be of service.

Forty-plus years have passed since my father's death and the choices I made to follow in his footsteps, and this I have learned along the way regarding funeral service and funeral business. You can join either, or sometimes both, but only both if you have a clear understanding that there is a difference. I have seen many fine funeral service professionals forget that there are two components to the profession. The "business" is what supports us as professionals. It gives us the means to provide for others what we have to offer to them. "Service" is what we give of ourselves, without thought of any type of personal gain, in order that those who suffer the loss of someone close, can move forward to new days. May it always be so.

If I have learned anything in my career in funeral service, it is the truth of these eloquent words from the late Maya Angelou, "I've learned that people will forget what you said, people will forget what you did. But people will never forget how you made them feel."

Funeral service is a worthy profession, filled with challenge and privilege, and built on trust.

*

CHASTIN BRINKLEY
Chastin is a 47-year-old funeral director, embalmer
and cremation specialist in Buckley, Washington

One day in elementary school, when I was with my friends on the playground, we were talking about our dads and their military service. When I told them my dad was in the Marine Corps, a couple of them laughed and said that the Marine Corps brainwashes you. That statement bothered me, and when I got home I told my mother what they said. She said they were right. The Marine Corps does brainwash you, they brainwash you to be the best. From that day forward I was going to be a marine.

My senior year came and I took the ASVAB Test (a military aptitude test) and physical for the marines. Afterward, my dad asked me what I was going to do for a career after serving. Up until that point, I had never thought about it. The Corps was going to be my life. It was during that time I was first introduced to funeral service when my best friend, who graduated a year earlier, started to work in a funeral home. He would tell me about interesting embalmings, as well as the visitations and funerals that followed. As the school year went on, I became more fascinated with funeral service to the point of asking what it takes to become an embalmer and funeral director. My friend introduced me to the funeral home manager and a funeral director and embalmer. They gave both of us valuable career advice and told us the dos and don'ts of mortuary school. Six months after I graduated high school, my friend received a job offer in Dallas, so we moved there with the goal of attending mortuary school. We graduated in 1991 and after serving my apprenticeship, I received my funeral director and embalming licenses in 1993.

*

JENNI BRYANT
Jenni is a 41-year-old funeral director
and embalmer in Maryville, Tennessee

After graduating from high school in 1993, I bounced back and forth between majors at the University of Tennessee in Knoxville for about five years. I started in architecture, but changed to early childhood education. I thought I had finally made my mind up when I decided to go to nursing school with a friend, who at the time was dating Josh, a funeral director. He would tell us stories, and talk about his day in a way that really intrigued me. Around January 1998, I decided to get more information from Josh about the funeral business. He told me where he went to school and that he really loved his job. The nursing program was in full swing, but I could not get the idea of mortuary school out of my head.

Then in March 1998, Josh was killed in a car accident. As I tried to comfort my friend after the loss of her boyfriend, I realized that I wanted to be more involved, more educated about death, grief, and loss. I felt that this was a sign for me. After talking with my parents, and my boyfriend at the time, who later became my husband, I began my own investigating. I called a few of the mortuary schools and decided to make a trip to Gupton-Jones in Atlanta in the fall of 1998. With the support of my family and friends, I moved to Decatur, Georgia, in February 1999 and enrolled in the mortuary science program at Gupton-Jones College.

I quickly knew that I had finally gotten it right! This was exactly what I wanted to be doing and school came pretty easy to me. I enjoyed going to class, learning and studying. I was a sponge, soaking up all I could about the funeral business. I found out that I was definitely not the normal student. Most of my classmates were second, third or even fourth generation funeral directors. They knew more about the funeral business than a few of our instructors. I enjoyed spending time with them and gaining some knowledge that I couldn't get in the classroom. I graduated with Honors in February 2000.

Shortly before graduation, I began the job hunt. I sent out over one hundred resumes and got two phone calls! I quickly realized how hard it was going to be to get a job as a woman in funeral service. One of the calls I got was from Don Gibson at Smith Funeral and Cremation Service. I went for my interview and was so impressed with this place! I knew this was where I wanted to begin my career.

Don offered me a position to do my apprenticeship, but guaranteed me a job for only one year. I started on the Monday after graduation, and this past February I celebrated sixteen years with Smith's.

I have come to realize that funeral service is very much a calling. Although I didn't realize it at the time, this was the path I was supposed to take. I have met some wonderful people, some not so wonderful people, and made some of the best friends I will ever have. I was lucky enough to find a firm to work for that is owned by two families who have taught me that being a funeral director is more than a job. It is an engaging career for people who love caring for others, learning new things, and honoring the aesthetics and meaning of life.

*

LAUREN BUDROW
Lauren is a 44-year-old funeral director
and funeral service educator

I have always said that funeral service found me and not the other way around. I was raised by an older generation of family members and consequently spent a significant time in my youth attending the funerals of great-aunts and uncles, and cousins. My earliest recollection of a funeral was my great-uncle Albert. I was about seven years old and I drew what I thought would be a consoling image of my uncle in a coffin (not casket) for his sister, my grandmother. Grandma graciously accepted the picture, not quite sure what to make of my decision to draw it. I believe that began my journey with what became my comfort and future career within the death care profession. I just didn't realize at that time there was such a thing as a funeral director. It never occurred to me to ask how my uncle ended up in his suit, lying in state for the family to see. He was simply dead and life was going on around him. In this way, I suppose I could say I grew up in a funeral home, but it wasn't because it was a family business. In fact, we were regular patrons, not owners, and somehow a career in funeral service didn't occur to me until much later.

At age twenty-eight, while between jobs and feeling quite lost professionally, my mother-in-law married a funeral director named Norman. My husband and I helped them move into a funeral home where they would live upstairs and then manage the sister firm a block down the street. Both funeral homes were owned by the same family. I felt completely at ease while we were moving furniture in and helping them get settled. Norm told hilarious stories about some of his years in funeral service and I started to consider funeral service as a possible career option. Since I was unemployed, I asked Norm to contact me when he had his first call so I could see what the job entailed. He called a week later and I was hooked.

For the next year, I commuted from Indianapolis to Vincennes University which was two and a half hours one way, two to three days a week. I stayed with my in-laws at the funeral home, which was halfway between the two, between travel days. That was what made completing my degree possible.

From Norm, I learned the power of storytelling and how important it is to let grieving families tell their stories. My family had been doing that all along but I didn't realize the value of it until I entered the profession. I began to see the significance of what they were doing in helping to remember and grieve for the many losses in our family. It was how we healed ourselves and carried on traditions. We would laugh as much as cry.

I have been in funeral service in some capacity for sixteen years. As a licensee I have met approximately 1,300 families, heard many stories and seen plenty of them unfold before my eyes. Oftentimes I would ask myself why such unbelievable circumstances would be happening to me with the families I was serving, and then I realized it was so I could relay those events to my future students and let them know that absolutely anything can happen to you in funeral service. I would tell them, "Learn from my mistakes from when I was a new funeral director, and don't let this happen to you." My students would regularly tell me that it was my stories that helped them remember what to do. I was continuing to serve families through my students.

I wouldn't trade my time in funeral service for anything. A friend pointed out that our profession is the only one that serves the living and the dead. What a privilege to be part of bridging the gap between both worlds while navigating the unpredictable waters of grief between them. A funeral director must be ready for anything to happen at any point following the death of a loved one. Society seems to have a love-hate relationship with us because they need our services but don't want them to be needed. In the end, we must answer all calls regardless of how we may be treated when we arrive.

*

JASON RYAN ENGLER
Jason is a 36-year-old funeral director, certified
celebrant, and cremation historian in Rogers, Arkansas

My interest in the funeral profession came at an early age, and my intrigue with the practice of cremation memorialization has made me somewhat of an expert in the subject. Though my interest in the funeral profession began at age twelve, it wasn't until 1996 when, barely sixteen, I went to work at a funeral home near my hometown of Seguin, Texas. I moved to Arkansas at age twenty, served my apprenticeship, and received my funeral director's license in 2003.

My interest has always been in taking care of families. I enjoy the creativity of making funerals personal for those who have lost loved ones. I find it very rewarding to be able to help those who are facing grief, so they may look back on the experience and, hopefully, have a positive memory of the event.

For me, funeral and memorial services are very ethereal in the way they relate our loved ones to us. I tend to focus on the memory of the deceased. A quote by writer Hugh Robert Orr in his poem "They Softly Walk" states my feelings exactly. He wrote, "They are not gone who pass beyond the clasp of hand, away from our strong embrace. They have but come so close we need not touch with hands, nor look to see, nor try to catch the sound of feet. They have taken off their shoes softly to walk by day within our thoughts, to tread at night our dream-led paths of sleep... They are not dead who live in hearts they leave behind." This poem has become my mantra. This is what funeral service is to me. Honoring memory, celebrating a life loved and lived, and helping the living make their way through their grief process.

I feel that our work does not only extend to the dead and the living that survive them, but also to colleagues who do what we do every day. Regardless of the reason, we all need encouragement and friendship, and I hope that when my friends and family gather to remember my life, they can say that I was a friend to all.

*

SHARON GEE-MASCARELLO
Sharon is a 53-year-old funeral director and embalming instructor
in the Mortuary Science Program at Wayne State University in Detroit

I was in grade school when I experienced my first death. I looked up from my desk at the same moment my mother looked in my classroom window. I read the bad news on her face. The door opened, she hugged me really hard, clasped my hand in hers, and whisked me to the car already laden with suitcases for our drive to Ashtabula, Ohio. We sat vigil at my grandfather's bedside for one extremely long day and huddled together as a family to watch my grandfather's body shut down. As his breathing grew increasingly shallow, we leaned forward on our chairs, straining to hear him until he pulled in one long breath and simply didn't exhale.

I was both saddened and fascinated by his death. After his funeral, I would rewind one scene: my mother uncovering her father's feet, cradling them in her hands and remarking how cold they felt. In retrospect, I recognize my fascination for the sciences.

In a brief span of two years I attended three more family funerals. My aunt was struck by a speeding motorist while crossing the street. Her sister, my paternal grandmother, suffered a stroke in her own bed, and her son (my father) died suddenly on Thanksgiving Day of a heart attack. He was forty-five and had celebrated his birthday just six days earlier. As he opened his present from me, I raised my camera to capture an expression of genuine surprise on his face. This is the last photograph I have of my father. I was thirteen. When I made it to the age of forty-five, I looked long and hard at that photo of my dad to see if I favored him. Yes, I do.

Fast forward to mortuary school when I was delivering a presentation to my classmates. The face of the school secretary appeared in the lecture room window. My mother had phoned the office to deliver news of her brother's (my uncle's) death by suicide. This time, there wasn't a bedside to attend. And, the casket remained closed. I wrote a poem for him instead. Several years later, his mother (my maternal grandmother) died of natural causes.

Many years passed. So many, that I felt safe thinking that death was held at arm's length. I concentrated my energies on funeral directing and teaching. When I made it to age forty-six, my very best friend, my mother, died of fourth stage lung cancer. I was a twenty-five-year veteran funeral director. It was my mother who urged me to take this leap of faith, to re-focus my own life. Perhaps I did so to honor my late family, to complete the collective unfinished business so to speak.

I left full-time funeral service the following year and added several new courses to my teaching load. Teaching affords me a great privilege. I am able to transfer my thirty-plus years of passion for funeral service onto new shoulders. I desire to focus my energy for the benefit of my students, to inspire and empower them to honorably and compassionately serve others. Recently, I shared with them the memorial tribute I had created for my mom. I smiled when they remarked how much I look like my mother. I recognized in their kind gestures, gentle tone of voice and tender facial expressions, that they were indeed funeral directors.

*

LOUISE GOHMANN
Louise is a 61-year-old mortuary school educator
and funeral director in Jeffersonville, Indiana

I began my career in the funeral industry as a door-to-door cemetery sales person. It was challenging to say the least, but I enjoyed it very much. My strangest sale was to a man who wanted to buy a mausoleum for his wife's fortieth birthday. I told him it might not be a good idea and maybe she might like some jewelry instead. He insisted it would be hilarious, and had me climb up a ladder to put a big red bow on it. It did not go well for him.

As I worked with more and more at-need families, I began to feel an inner nudge to look into becoming a funeral director. The nudge became a push, and before I knew it I was enrolled in mortuary school. I am what they call a nontraditional, multi-career student. I was the only grandmother in my class. I relished my new position.

I anticipated on-call nights like a firedog ready for action. My husband was supportive but concerned about the idea of my dashing out in the middle of the night. At first he insisted on getting up with me and waiting until I got home. It wasn't too long, though, before he got used to the idea. Now I get an elbow in my back and a muttered, "Your phone's ringing," as he rolls over in bed.

Being a funeral director is one of the most rewarding, frustrating, and enlightening careers I know of. I've laughed out loud with families as they share stories of their loved ones, and stood with tears in my eyes while helping a mother close the casket of her child. I've cherished my years as a funeral director, with all of its ups and downs. My career was in funeral service and I didn't expect to deviate from that path. When I took a teaching position at Mid-America College of Funeral Service, my plans headed in a completely different direction. As the late Yogi Berra said, "When you come to a fork in the road, take it!" I discovered the joy—literally—of teaching. I transitioned from being a full-time funeral director to teaching tomorrow's funeral directors. Hopefully I am able to foster in them the same passion and compassion I have for funeral service. I believe that I am a good resource for my students, because I am in the trenches right alongside them as I continue to work at a local funeral home.

*

KAREN JELLY
Karen is a 44-year-old funeral director
and mortician in Havre, Montana

In 2001, I began working for a local funeral home as the office manager, putting to use my business degree. While there, I discovered that my love for helping others was fulfilled in my professional life as well as my personal life. I remained the office manager for over two years, when, at our mortician's urging, I began preparing for mortuary school. I served an apprenticeship in Wyoming, and an internship in Montana before finally becoming licensed, however the experience I gained during both has helped me tremendously. Since 2001, I have remained in this line of work off and on.

In 2012, my family and I moved to Havre, Montana, where I have been working full-time (plus) as a funeral director in a small town, family-owned funeral home. I graduated from mortuary school in 2012 as well, and began the licensing process. I became fully licensed in 2013, and have remained here to serve the residents and the many friends I have made in my new hometown.

Since the summer of 2013, I have gained considerable experience, as my friend and manager was in a terrible automobile accident, resulting in a traumatic brain injury. This left me as the only fully licensed funeral director here that could work. We did have an intern for a year, but he moved on after he became licensed.

When people ask me why I became a funeral director, I explain to them that it is like being a social worker without having to break up families. I come into a person's life at one of the most difficult times, and help them get through the frustration and details, so that they can begin to heal.

Please don't think that the emotional trauma families go through does not affect us. On the contrary, it affects us significantly. We feel a portion of their pain, and try to ease it. In small towns, we often care for those we knew, and because of that, experience loss as well. Through it all, we remain strong and steady for the families, because that is what they need at that time.

Sometimes, we get to know people we had not yet met, and in caring for their family members, they become friends—people we remain close to for many years to come. Often, when I have cared for someone's loved one, they will avoid me for a time when seeing me out in public. I am a reminder of a painful time in their life, so we are often not the most popular of people.

A few years ago I was asked if, knowing what I know now about the industry, I would do it all over again? I responded immediately with yes. Yes, some days I come to work with less than three hours of sleep. Yes, some days I take care of people I knew, and in doing so, I hurt. Yes, some days families are not cooperative, and some days, they are downright combative. But yes, I would do it all over again!

*

CODY JONES
Cody is a 37-year-old progressive funeral home owner
and funeral director in Bryan-College Station, Texas

I grew up in Bryan, Texas, as the only son of Michael D. and Lorene Jones. Ours is a family of funeral professionals. Our business was founded five generations ago, in 1904 in Palestine, Texas. During my high school years, I observed the business firsthand and began helping out at a very early age. It was the family business, so wearing a suit and going to the office with my dad and mom was just like anyone else, or so I thought.

In our Callaway-Jones family, the women had been leaders as well as full business partners alongside their husbands from the beginning. My great-grandfather, Homer Callaway, had been working for Frank Bailey Furniture and Undertaking in 1904 when he married Miss Sallye Lacy. He graduated from the Philadelphia School of Embalmers and was licensed as our family's first funeral director in 1907. He and Sallye had three children while building their business. She ultimately graduated as a licensed Texas funeral director and embalmer.

As parents to sons Lester and Ramon, and daughter Homer Lacy, they relocated to Crockett, Texas, where they established Callaway Furniture and Undertaking. It seemed natural that the furniture business operated downstairs and the undertaking business operated upstairs. A superb entrepreneur, Sallye also opened the first floral shop in Crockett. I heard the stories while growing up, and felt especially proud that the Callaway-Jones family had also established a formal burial association, the first of its kind in Texas. Ultimately it operated from 1930 to 1968, when it became the Callaway Life Insurance Company.

Because her mother was an undertaker, my great-grandmother, Homer Lacy Callaway, married Manley Jones in Crockett. Homer too became a licensed funeral director, and Manley joined his wife in the profession, which is how we reached the business and building that I grew up in: Callaway-Jones Funeral Home, established in 1953 on

College Avenue in Bryan, where it stood for the next sixty years. Their two sons, Raymond Callaway Jones and Manley Wright Jones Jr., grew up in First United Methodist Church of Bryan.

Raymond, my grandfather, grew up around Texas A&M and was the first in the family to attend Aggieland. At the time, A&M was all-male enrollment and required mandatory membership in the TAMU Corps of Cadets. In 1953, he earned a Bachelor's degree in accounting and the next year earned his funeral director's license. At age twenty-four, he became co-owner of Callaway-Jones Funeral Home.

He remained in the Brazos Valley, married his high school sweetheart, and both became members of A&M United Methodist Church. I grew up knowing my grandparents, and understood how important the business was to them. Equally important was being part of our community. My grandfather provided free ambulance service at all the Aggie home football games and never missed a game. He also loved the College Station Kiwanis Club, and was past president of the Better Business Bureau of the Brazos Valley. He was also a Mason member for fifty-two years. He was considered a legend in the funeral industry for all that he accomplished, but awards didn't mean as much to him as time spent with his family. Family was always first.

When my dad, Michael D. Jones, was growing up, I'm sure he was expected to enter the family business to continue it on. If he ever considered a different career, he never spoke of it. He met Lorene, my mom, when she was studying accounting at Texas A&M. When she graduated with her degree in 1977, she worked in Houston for a while but Dad pursued her. They married and made their home in Bryan-College Station. They were active in the A&M Methodist Church he had grown up in.

When my father became co-owner of the business with my grandparents, he was only twenty-four. Lorene joined the business, too. Together, they built the company at College Avenue on honest, genuine care for families. Other funeral homes existed in town but competition was never a concern nor did they fear being bad-mouthed by another business. It was a very small community, so we were all friends. That was before the creation of mega-corporations, some of whose practices and prices didn't appeal to our hometown folks. We watched but we weren't worried.

Mom and Dad worked side by side. Lorene became a licensed funeral director, crematory operator, and insurance agent just as Sallye Callaway had joined her husband at work. Together, they did it all. I must say that while growing up, I was never pressured to join the business. Nothing my parents said ever made me feel like I had to follow their footsteps. They knew I loved being outdoors. Dad taught me how to play golf, a sport I still love today. My dad was also our soccer coach. My parents drove us all over the country to compete in tournaments. They established a soccer league here in Texas, and created our own tournament which is still active today. The local soccer fields were renamed in my father's honor when he passed.

Life was a lot of fun for me when it came time to choose a college. I grew up in Bryan, graduated from Bryan High School, and took classes at Texas A&M while still in high school. But they didn't have exactly what I was looking for, which was mostly to get out of town. I enrolled at Southern Methodist University, SMU, in Dallas, where I studied marketing and communications. There I also found that I had a real love for graphic arts, and computers were fun. I didn't even entertain the thought of going into the family business.

After SMU, I pursued graduate studies in Los Angeles. I loved surfing, and found that working on graphic arts and animation projects was the best thing I'd ever done to bring me joy. But then my father was diagnosed with leukemia. He was such a young man. To know that he couldn't work alongside his dad while in treatment was hard on him. He and my grandfather were best friends.

I had a choice to make, but it didn't take long. I moved back to Texas and began working with my grandfather while Dad was battling cancer. My mom still worked at the business and was there for every treatment with my dad. When I came back to town, I had some innovative ideas though they would have to wait while I relearned the business. I was twenty-four when I began working with my grandfather, the same age he and my dad both began.

Our business was established in a vintage 1953 building. We'd long outgrown the size of the building, and so the race was on. Big funeral corporations entered our market and bought local homes. But I was a fighter and determined to protect our business, plus grow it larger. Challenges were many. Our building was old, the inside looked worn and tired, and we needed more space—fast.

I was lucky to meet my wife, Chelsea, and she quickly became my partner in work while she also had a second independent career. Lorene, my mother, continues to manage our accounting and whatever we need. Together, I'm proud of our amazing team, who are family to us. They are the real secret of our success; their devotion and dedication to our family is unparalleled.

We were blessed when the neighboring St. Michael's Academy allowed us to use their chapel for funerals during construction of our new funeral center. The community faithfully stayed with us when construction took longer than expected. Our new funeral center now has amazing space with ample natural light, giving it a warm, comforting atmosphere. We even have a cremation suite. We're new, and yet we're the same family team who have been part of the community for generations.

The job of a funeral director is to bring calm, peace, respect, organization and strength to those who are grieving the loss of their loved one. Although it was not my original career choice, I'm so glad to be here in my community, proof that you don't have to be a huge corporation to heal hearts in pain. Every day I carry the hopes and dreams of five generations in my heart as I work to develop innovations for the future. Perhaps one day, my future children will want to join me. You never know.

*

CORIANN MARTIN
Coriann is a 42-year-old funeral director
and embalmer in Kenosha, Wisconsin

We all have those defining moments in life. The ones that have a lasting impact, the driving force behind what led you to believe that this is your passion, this is what you were destined to be. Well, I don't have one of those stories. I was a typical child; I didn't experience much trauma in life. The only losses I suffered were losing grandparents or relatives who I was too young to remember or didn't have the closest relationships with.

I guess if I had to blame anyone for giving me the idea to look into a career that seemed so far outside the box for a four-foot eleven-inch female to enter, the award would have to go to my high school biology teacher. He was my favorite teacher and during class he would share stories about his younger years helping out at a local funeral home. Something about his stories intrigued me and I figured if I could dissect earthworms and crayfish, how different could it be with humans? So, I went for it and started planning my education to concentrate on science-based classes. After completing prerequisite courses at a college away from home to experience on-campus living, I returned home and waited for my opportunity to apply to the technical college that offered an associate's degree in mortuary science.

Fast forwarding through two years of school, a year-long apprenticeship, summer internships, state boards, and five funeral homes, I am working in a career that I love. It wasn't an easy path;

there were long hours. It's a mentally and physically demanding job, but I can't see myself doing anything else. The people you meet professionally, and the families you serve that you never lose touch with, make the hard times that much more tolerable.

I had a moment in my past that I questioned my decision. I left the industry for six months when my life collided with getting married, moving, leaving a funeral home I loved, all in one month. Readjusting to a new life with a husband, a new home, living in an unfamiliar city and working in a new funeral home was just too much. I tried "normal" for a little while. I worked a nine-to-five job, no nights, no weekends. It hit me that when I was out in public and people asked me the typical, "What do you do for a living?" question, I was embarrassed to tell them what I did. I found a sense of pride telling people that I was a funeral director. I returned to the same funeral home I left and picked up right where I left off. It's been sixteen years and I couldn't be happier.

*

JENNIFER PARKS
Jennifer is a 45-year-old certified funeral
celebrant in Santa Barbara, California

It all began with baby Remington. Remi was a full-term baby who, twelve hours after he was born, died in his mother's arms from a very rare complication of pregnancy called maternal-fetal hemorrhage. At the time I managed the mortuary. Sitting with families was not one of my responsibilities, until fate stepped in and put me in Remi, Kellie and Christian's path.

A series of events led me to be the one to sit with this family and bear witness to their utter devastation. They asked if they could see their boy. They said that the events that led up to her emergency cesarean, and his passing, were terribly chaotic and they didn't feel as if they had a chance to say a proper goodbye. The only answer I could give was one from a mother's heart, because I had no experience to base it on. I told them I would go get their son from the hospital and if he looked like their beautiful baby, then, yes I would prepare a place for them to spend as much time with him as they needed.

Then they said that the memorial prints that the hospital had given them of Remi's hands and feet looked like they had been done on Post-it notes. They asked if I would do them again, and if I could take impressions in clay. I said yes. Those impressions of tiny perfect feet and tiny perfect hands took me hours to do. I rolled and rerolled that clay until the impressions were perfect. This was the only physical representation that these parents would have that their son was here.

It was in the preparation of baby Remi's body, and the care of his mom and dad, when I learned I was destined for this work. In those first moments of assisting the family on this very personal journey of overwhelming love and unspeakable loss, I knew this was my calling.

I had the privilege of working with seasoned funeral directors and an extraordinarily talented, artistic embalmer that gave me the gift of their time and talents and taught me everything they knew so that I could answer this calling. I took the courses needed to satisfy the requirements of the state. Then, I sat with those families in need and

I listened, I made suggestions, I made arrangements and I helped them honor the person they loved and lost.

Whenever I make arrangements now, Remi is never far from my thoughts. He reminds me that "To the world you may be one person but to one person you may be the world." I'm lucky to work in a profession whose only objective is to be of service, and to stand bravely alongside grief and say, "I am here. I will take care of you."

*

LACY ROBINSON
Lacy is a 38-year-old Director of Member Development for the
National Funeral Directors Association in Brookfield, Wisconsin

The year 1993 was life-changing for me. I was in the eighth grade and my grandfather died of cancer. I remember every detail of that entire experience from what my grandmother wore to the funeral to the "Going Home" embroidered casket panel.

Following his death, my other grandfather died from a stroke. Again I remember every single detail. I remember the female funeral director who helped me place a letter in my grandfather's suit jacket and walked alongside with her arm around me at the cemetery. It was both of those funerals that triggered a desire to learn more about funeral service. After those two events, every high school project and research assignment that came my way, I always made it about funeral service. Whether it was researching the chemical composition of formaldehyde to early American funeral customs, my teachers came to expect my homework assignments to stand out from others. The summer before my senior year of high school I walked down the street to the funeral home and asked if I could have a job. After that summer, my dream was to become a funeral director.

*

SHAWNA RODABAUGH
Shawna is a 37-year-old funeral director and
embalmer in Mount Pleasant, Michigan

As a young child, my father, who was a biologist, nourished my interest in science. We would spend long afternoons in the woods behind our home, exploring the nature around us and taking in everything it had to offer. At the age of eleven, I had my first encounter with death, losing a close friend to natural causes. Seeing her at the funeral affected me greatly at such a young age, and piqued my interest in the science of death care, giving those who have lost dear ones the opportunity to say goodbye to them.

I spent my schooling and apprentice years focused on the act of giving families the opportunity to see and grieve their loved ones, regardless of circumstance. At funeral services, people tend to say things along the lines of, "If there's anything I can do, let me know." As a funeral director, I feel I am in the unique position to provide something that in some ways will ease the pain of losing a loved one. I can give them their loved one back for a brief time, to say goodbye, and to begin the process of grieving.

After spending ten years in traditional funeral service, I began to feel called to education. There are many ways for families to find meaning in death, and one of those ways is through anatomical donation. This allows families an opportunity to build the education of young healthcare workers in several fields, in a real, tangible way. With the gift given to our students, I feel honored to be the one to represent, care for and advocate for the donors at my university. Part of my work is to ensure that the students remember the incredible gift they have received, and to offer them opportunities to express their gratitude to the families with our annual donor recognition.

Although there have been a few nontraditional turns in my career, the science of death care to me will always be about assisting families in finding what is meaningful to them once they've lost someone they love. Whether that is a traditional funeral, donation, or anything in between, it is an honor to be a part of it.

*

STEVE TWEEDLE
Steve is a 42-year-old funeral
director in Ocala, Florida

I started working at the funeral home when I was fifteen. One of the first families we met when we moved to the area from Miami was the Baxley family. Dennis Baxley was the town funeral director. Our families became very close as I was growing up. My sister and I were close in age to the Baxley kids, and we spent many hours together. I remember running around the funeral home when I was a child, playing hide-and-seek in between the pews of the chapel, and learning what all the different switches, knobs and pedals do on an organ.

When I started working, at fifteen, I was responsible for the lawn. I would catch a ride to the funeral home after school, knock on the window of the office, and Maudie, the secretary, would give me the go-ahead if it was okay to work. I did the lawn for about two years, and then it was time for me to graduate high school. I had been accepted to the University of Florida and I wanted to be an architect. I needed a car and money, so I had to quit the funeral home (twenty-five dollars a week does not cover tuition to the University of Florida). My grandfather was the town pharmacist and got me a job at the pharmacy he worked at.

Belleview, Florida is a small town. When someone wants to talk to you, there's no avoiding it. I had heard through the grapevine that Dennis Baxley wanted me to come back to work for the funeral home. That grapevine was, of course, my parents. Dennis had called and left several messages for me, asking me to call him back, and I was avoiding him. He needed an associate, someone to work closely with the funeral director assisting on funerals, bringing people under our care from hospitals and homes, and keeping the inside of the building clean. I didn't want anything to do with the funeral home. Being a child hiding under pews is one thing; touching dead people—something else entirely.

One of the aspects of being a good funeral director is tenacity. You work hard with the family, learning about them and their loved one. You need to organize the minister, funeral escorts, the cemetery, vocalist and musicians. You have to be determined that things are going to go the way they are planned. No one ever told me that about funeral directors.

I came home from college one day, and as I pulled into the driveway, Dennis Baxley's car was sitting in the spot I normally parked my car...tenacity. So I went into the house and there he was at the dining room table talking to my dad. I was trapped. All he wanted me to do was listen to what he had to say. I had a very accomplished salesperson tell me one time, "I don't want to talk to someone who is going to buy. I want to talk to someone who is going to listen." At first that didn't make sense, but he was right.

Dennis described the work: "You'll help us on funerals, you'll move flowers, you'll be responsible for keeping the building clean, you'll need to keep the vehicles spotless... and you'll need to help us with removals." Even as a layperson, I knew what that meant and I wasn't so sure I wanted to do that part. At the end he talked about compensation and assured me they would work around my schooling. Because of the way the work schedule happened to be, I was basically working a full-time job even though I wasn't physically in the building, and going to school full-time. As a student, it's hard to turn down full-time pay while not putting in full-time hours. We were expected, and paid, to be available at all times.

Again, I was going to the University of Florida, driving to and from Gainesville every day. The 1984 Celebrity station wagon that I inherited from my parents was nowhere near cool enough for an eighteen-year-old college student, and tuition was due. I accepted the position purely for monetary reasons. So I went to the local Belk department store and bought my first suit. I can remember asking the associate at the store to help me match a tie to the suit; I had no clue what I was doing. Little did I know that this was the very beginning of my journey.

When I got inside, I did what I was asked. I kept the cars clean, I cleaned toilets, I dusted the tables, I vacuumed, and vacuumed, and vacuumed. Some days it felt like all I did was vacuum. But as the days went on, I started to realize that what we were doing wasn't about manual work. Here was a group of people who had dedicated their life to taking care of someone's most precious gift: a mother, a father, a brother, a sister, a child. They did it without asking questions, without being judgmental, without complaint, without worrying about themselves. So for me it became less about doing what I was supposed to do, but doing what I could for the family who was coming in that day to make arrangements, or the people who would be coming in for the visitation that night. Mr. Baxley would always say, "It's about service. What can I do to serve?" That's why when people ask me about this profession if they think they want to be a funeral director, I always tell them that they don't get to pick this job, this job picks them.

*

BRIAN VAN HECK
Brian is a 41-year-old funeral director in
the Lake Norman area of North Carolina

At the age of seven, the seeds of funeral directing were planted in my young mind. Our elderly neighbor, Mr. Logeman, was diagnosed with terminal cancer in a time when hospice and in-home health care was not what it is today. My mother, a nurse, offered that she, my dad and I would go across the street every night after dinner to provide care to Mr. Logeman. While my mom took care of the medical and physical aspects of his care, my dad and I took care of the emotional aspect, watching Pittsburgh Pirates baseball games with him and simply visiting.

After several weeks of the nightly hospice visits, Mr. Logeman died. I was there the night he left his earthly home and distinctly remember the two gentlemen in dark suits backing their white hearse into the driveway. They respectfully transferred the body of Mr. Logeman from the bed onto their cot and into the back of the hearse, slowly pulling away once he was secure.

Over the next few days I grew more intrigued with the role and responsibility of the funeral director. Mr. Logeman's funeral was held at the Presbyterian church he and his wife attended. The funeral director allowed me to hand out memorial folders to the guests as they entered the church while he seated them, so that the 11 a.m. funeral could start promptly, as I would learn later a good funeral director does. Upon conclusion of the funeral ceremony, Mark, the funeral director, approached and asked if I would like to ride in the hearse on the way to the cemetery. Enthusiastically, yet with some trepidation, I asked my mom if that would be alright; my intrigue with this whole funeral process was continuing to grow further yet. I remember glancing back often, looking through the glass which literally separated the living (driver and passenger) from the dead and seeing Mr. Logeman's flag-draped casket. Mark and I respectfully led the funeral procession from the church to the cemetery.

Once at the cemetery the minister led us in some prayers and scripture readings before turning the service over to the military. Mr. Logeman had served in the United States Army during World War II and was therefore eligible for Military Funeral Honors. After the volley of the rifles (more commonly known as the twenty-one gun salute), and the playing of taps, the military honor team respectfully and methodically folded the flag into the traditional triangle shape. They then turned to ME and presented ME with our United States flag that had adorned Mr. Logeman's casket. As I pen the words to this reflection, that very flag is housed in a wooden and glass case on a credenza behind the desk in my office. As the men in uniform stood in front of me and saluted me, I was wide-eyed. I have come to term my whole experience surrounding Mr. Logeman's death as my positive death experience at the young age of seven. The death and funeral of Clarence "Clem" Paul Logeman forever changed my life. It planted the seed of funeral directing as a career in which I could minister to families in a time of great need, honor the dead as a life well lived, and serve my community… each notable in their own right.

Years rolled on, and as a boy attending Catholic school, I had the opportunity to get out of class to serve in the role of altar boy on many funerals. Admittedly, the compensation package of getting out of class, the two to five-dollar salary and a decent meal after the cemetery was a huge motivating factor; but aside from that, there was the awe and fascination with the rituals and ceremony of the funeral. In that, I noticed individuals who were involved who seemed to artfully and eloquently orchestrate the various elements. These individuals were the funeral directors. Ironically, perhaps more appropriately divinely, the funeral director I was serving with most often was the funeral director from Mr. Logeman's funeral years earlier. I vividly recall serving one funeral with my friend Mike, as we were riding in the backseat of the lead car in the funeral procession from the church to the cemetery. Mike and I looked at one another and said, "We're going to be funeral directors when we get older." While I have upheld my end of our fifth grade vow, Mike has gone on and become an engineer.

Life progressed after the fifth grade and while I believe thoughts of being a funeral director were always there, my journey took some unique twists and turns before achieving my mortuary science license (state of Michigan). During my junior year of undergraduate studies, I contacted a funeral director in my hometown of Grand Rapids, Michigan, expressing my interest in the profession. After a lengthy conversation, I hung up the phone feeling discouraged because the gentleman had dissuaded me from entering the profession and was negative about the future of the role of funeral directors. As a result, I spent countless hours of personal reflection and discussions with professionals in related fields, and realized that I had a strong desire and drive to help people in time of great need, specifically as they experience the death loss of a loved one.

My realization led me to pursue a Master's in counseling and eventually doctoral education and training in counseling psychology. Having a solid sense of identity in regards to my area of interest, I searched for a program that would allow me to foster and develop in the area of bereavement, death and dying. In so doing, I was able to partner with a licensed psychologist who had a company that established bereavement aftercare programs for funeral homes throughout the country. In my first semester of graduate studies, this gentleman gave me a part-time job in a multi-location funeral home, which gave me my first real experience in funeral service.

It has been nearly twenty years since the first time I transferred a deceased from the place of death, set up flowers for a visitation, parked and washed the professional vehicles (hearse, lead car, and limousine), and I can say with absolute certainty that being a funeral director and working in funeral service is my professional home. My educational and professional journey, while not the most direct path to becoming a funeral director, was and continues to be very rewarding. God brought, and continues to bring, many wonderful people into my life, from educators, mentors and most importantly the families I am so honored to serve. I will be forever grateful.

*

KIMBERLY VARELA
Kimberly is a 41-year-old funeral director
and embalmer in Westland, Michigan

Through a very long route I found my way back to an original calling I had in my twenties. My interests in science, especially

35

anatomy and biology, led me down a road in the medical field. Through an interesting set of circumstances, I found myself employed as an airfreight logistics specialist moving cargo from the United States to all over the world. I spent close to fifteen years in this fast-paced field but after 9/11, the industry and economy drastically changed. I was unemployed and decided to make a life change.

I went back to college at thirty-one years old and completed my degree in mortuary science. I loved it from the very beginning. Part of me wishes I had obtained my degree earlier, but I feel my life experiences and maturity help me every day. The recent loss of several close family members in a short period of time has added to my level of empathy and insight from both sides of the arrangement table.

*

DAN WELCH
Dan is a 30-year-old funeral director and
embalmer in Wichita, Kansas

In 1996, I stood by the casket of my great-grandmother in a cold, dungy and outdated funeral home just outside Lincoln, Nebraska. I remember looking at my great-grandmother and not recognizing her. I left that night feeling as though I had attended the funeral of a stranger, and fear swept over me. That was my first exposure to death; there was so much unknown, and it scared me.

Fast forward to 1998. I found myself standing next to the casket of my brother's dear friend. I had become petrified at the idea of being in the same room as a dead body. I left that funeral before it even started, and sat in the car by myself until the services were complete. Yet again, the fear of the unknown had overtaken me, so much so that I was losing sleep over the issue. My parents sent me to a therapist to process my fear. We never really found the root of it.

In 2008, while finishing my bachelor's degree at a bible college, I heard that the grief and dying class was going to tour a local funeral home. Even though I was not a part of the class, the curiosity behind funeral service and death was something I wanted to explore. I had reached a point in life when I had allowed the fear of death and funerals to control me, and I figured the more I could learn about it, the more I would be able to conquer any fear associated with it.

The tour at the funeral home was less than impressive and I didn't get much out of it. However, the one thing I took away from the funeral director was the desire for him and his colleagues to allow families to be involved in all aspects of the funeral—whether that meant assisting with the removal, dressing their loved one, making the service folders, and so on. His thought was that all of those acts are ways for families to begin the healing process after losing a loved one.

Several months after the tour of the funeral home, I found myself standing at the bedside of my deceased grandfather. When the funeral directors arrived from the neighboring town, they clearly maintained the same philosophy as the funeral directors from the establishment I had toured months earlier. Without hesitation the funeral director looked at me and asked if I would like to assist with transferring my grandfather into their care. I gladly assisted and was instantly honored to be able to care for my grandfather in that way. The funeral director recognized how much this meant to me, and during the arrangement conference the next day, I was asked if I wanted to assist with dressing and casketing my grandfather. I was astounded by the idea that I would be able to take care of my grandfather in this way.

The next day I arrived to the funeral home and assisted with the final preparation of my grandfather. I stood there and watched the care and dignity the funeral director had toward my grandfather as we dressed him together. He was so compassionate toward him; every movement was methodical and respectful. Within thirty minutes, grandpa looked better than he had looked in years and it was all because of this funeral director's actions.

I left the funeral home that day with a new respect for funeral directors. For years I believed the Hollywood lies that they were cold-hearted scam artists who were out to make a quick buck. I learned they were so far from that—they were actually servants and ministers.

Following the visitation of my grandfather, I stuck around the funeral home and picked the brain of the funeral director. I wanted to know everything there was to know about funeral service. Time obviously was not on our side that night, but the director was able to get me in contact with a funeral director back in my hometown. A few short weeks after my grandfather's funeral, I contacted the funeral home in my hometown and began a dialogue with the funeral director about the profession. We sat and spoke for nearly two hours. By the end of the conversation, I was an employee of the funeral home. I left not knowing what had happened, but was excited to learn more.

Over the next seven months, I spent every spare moment at the funeral home. I was a sponge. I wanted to learn as much as I possibly could as quickly as I possibly could. What had once been a dreaded fear of mine as a child had quickly turned into a new obsession of learning. I completely surrounded myself with everything pertaining to funeral service. I was blessed to have the opportunity to help with every facet of funeral service—everything from dressing bodies to working funeral services. I did it all and I loved it all. It was something that I could see myself doing for many years to come, however I felt as though I was missing something. I finally discovered what the something was on a late February night.

That was a night I'll never forget, and one I've played through my head thousands of times. It's the night I remind myself of when feeling burned out or when a death call comes in at 3:30 a.m. That night changed my life's path, and was when I received the calling funeral directors speak of when they talk about working in the profession.

I sat alone at the funeral home that evening for nearly three hours without a single person crossing the threshold. We had two bodies lying in state that evening. Both of them had scheduled visitation times for the next day, however it was customary at this firm to stay open until 8 p.m. every night if a body was dressed and in state in the off-chance that the family may want to come by. That off-chance happened to me that evening.

About five minutes before I was to close, a lady in her mid-thirties came walking through the door. I did not recognize her but she quickly introduced herself as Damion's mother. My heart stopped because I knew that Damion was the nine-year-old who was killed in the housefire days earlier and was one of the decedents lying in state. Here standing before me was a grieving mother coming in to see her deceased son for the first time—by herself.

I offered my condolences to her and politely offered to take her to the room where Damion was lying in state. As we walked down the hallway she began to softly cry. As we got to the door I slowly opened it and told her to take as much time as she needed. Our eyes locked for just a moment before she cried out, "Please go in there with me!" Without a moment of hesitation, I put my arms around her and assured her I would be by her side.

Unfortunately, we never made it completely into the room that night. As the door opened the remainder of the way, she caught a glimpse of her son for the first time lying in the casket some twenty feet inside the room. For the next hour and a half I stood there with a stranger, holding her in a tight hug as she wailed. It was a cry I will never forget—a deep, guttural moan that only a person who has lost a child will probably ever fully understand. It was a cry that I have never heard since that night, and honestly, a cry I hope I never hear again. But that cry, that moment, was when I finally knew that funeral service was my calling—my true ministry I could offer to people when they were in their deepest of valleys.

That night when I finally made it home, I told my wife how I felt it was necessary to step down at our church and pursue funeral service full time. By the grace of God, she was fully supportive, as was the rest of my family and friends. A few short months later, I found myself enrolled at mortuary school and working for one of the largest embalming services in the country.

Over the next year, I made it my goal to be the best in everything I did, knowing that someday thousands of families would count on my professionalism and expertise. I graduated with a 4.0 grade point average and had nearly two hundred embalmings under my belt prior to receiving my diploma. Upon graduation, I felt the desire to come back and serve the people of my community. It is here that I have served as a full-time funeral director, embalmer and certified crematory operator for the last five years.

*

A FUNERAL DIRECTOR'S PRAYER
Anthony J. Asselta

Lord, give me the patience needed
to serve everyone as my own;
the wisdom to understand other's feelings;
the knowledge to learn as well as to instruct;
the kindness to treat everyone equally at all times;
the strength to endure long hours and hard work;
the desire to serve others as I would my own family;
the humility to accept words of thanks and praise;
the compassion to touch another's soul;
the pride and the right to smile
when I have served a family well;
and Lord, most importantly the right to shed
an honest tear when my heart is touched;
Lord, make me thankful that
I am a Funeral Director.

*

CHAPTER TWO

The Big Decision

It is in your moments of decision that
your destiny is shaped. -TONY ROBBINS

Decision-making is the act of choosing between two or more action, either by intuitive or a reasoned process. For some, the decision to work in the funeral industry was easy. For others, the path wasn't as straight. When did you know you wanted to work in the funeral industry? Was the decision easy or hard?

*

STEPHEN BARON
Stephen is a 64-year-old funeral service
licensee in Grand Haven, Michigan

Growing up in a funeral home gives one a unique childhood and it presents one with rare opportunities to get acquainted with your parents' work. Having said that, I suppose there was a part of my being that sensed that I too may one day be a larger part of the activities that surrounded me daily. That and my close relationship with my dad as I was growing up, somewhat made it very clear that funeral service was always a real choice for me. These facts also gave me a firsthand look at the downside of the profession. This was a chance not given to most of us looking from the outside in. So, my first love affair with the job came at a very young age.

None of what brought me to this career choice was immediate, but it all very much played its part in the end choice. As a young child, from about six to age thirteen, it was all I wanted to do career wise. Know that I looked at it all through the eyes of a kid. For example, I had a deep interest in the "rolling stock," the livery, simply the cars. By age eight, I could identify the chassis and coachwork manufacturer, give the year it was made, and whether it was a "three-way" or "rear load" from the distance of a city block. The things that showed readily on the outside of the profession were the intrigue.

At age eighteen, following my father's death, I began to look at things with a career in mind. It would not be for another two years when I pursued the career, and only after weighing many pros and cons and taking an inventory of just where I would fit into all of this. The thing I struggled with most was the time commitment required by this job. There are no set hours for this job, and in smaller funeral homes you often put other parts of your life in a secondary position.

I guess for me the decision was immediate. It just took me several years to commit.

*

CHASTIN BRINKLEY
Chastin is a 47-year-old funeral director, embalmer
and cremation specialist in Buckley, Washington

I was seventeen when I decided to be a funeral director and embalmer. I didn't tell my parents right away because I was not sure how they would react. They had set aside some money over the years with the intention of using it for my education. However, a few years prior, I had shocked my parents when I told them I was not going to college because I was going into the Marine Corps. I suggested they use the college money for my sister.

Toward the end of my senior year in high school, I told my parents I was going to mortuary school. They didn't know what to think. This all seemed sudden to my folks, and they thought my high school buddy had way too much influence over me. My parents simply did not realize how much thought or planning I had put into my decision. For example, my friend and I needed an apartment in the near future. So, we thought, why not buy furnishings to prepare? When there was a sale at the mall on bath towels, dishes or any household items, we would buy them, take them to my friend's house and store them in his basement. One gas station in town gave a free drinking glass with each fill-up. Eventually we had enough items to furnish our apartment. I had even purchased my first suit, shirt and ties, giving my parents the impression they were for church. After I revealed all of this to my parents, they became very supportive.

*

JENNI BRYANT
Jenni is a 41-year-old funeral director
and embalmer in Maryville, Tennessee

I was twenty-four when I knew I wanted to work in the funeral industry. After talking with my parents, and my boyfriend at the time who later became my husband, I began my own investigating. I called a few of the mortuary schools and decided to make a trip to Gupton-Jones in Atlanta in the fall of 1998. In February 1999, with the support of family and friends, I moved to Decatur, Georgia, and enrolled in the mortuary science program at Gupton-Jones College. I was nervous about going to school—I had never seen a dead body.

*

LAUREN BUDROW
Lauren is a 44-year-old funeral director
and funeral service educator

Once I realized being a funeral director was the career I wanted, the decision was immediate. I enrolled in mortuary school less than a month later because I realized that was where I felt I belonged. I was twenty-eight years old. The only emotion I felt was complete excitement for having found my career path. I wanted to know everything possible about funeral service and attitudes surrounding it. When I told my family, they were surprised but then said it seemed like the perfect fit for me. My parents were supportive but did not always want to know details of some of what I was learning.

*

JASON RYAN ENGLER
Jason is a 36-year-old funeral director, certified celebrant,
and cremation historian in Rogers, Arkansas

My first interest of wanting to be a funeral director goes to about third grade, when I was eight years old. Though funerals had always been a part of my life (I remember several, including those of family members, pets and even GI Joe figures), they really began to interest me when my stepmom took our family across the state of Texas one summer to research family history for her involvement in the Daughters of the Republic of Texas. In the process, we spent countless hours in cemeteries taking photographs of family members' graves. My interest in cemeteries began there. Over the next several years, I pestered my dad to drive by the cemeteries and funeral homes in our hometown. One day when we were driving by a cemetery, he stated, "Jason, since you are so interested in cemeteries, why don't you become an undertaker?"

When I was twelve, I became interested in professional wrestling. It was 1992, and a wrestler called The Undertaker was an enigmatic character in wrestling television. His manager, Paul Bearer, intrigued me. He wore dark suits, carried an urn, and looked like what I thought a funeral director would look like. I wanted to be like him!

From there, my interest blossomed into admiration and pursuance of the profession of funeral directing. Though at first my parents were concerned about my morbid curiosity, I suppose they saw in me an earnestness and compassion in caring for others.

I'll admit that, in looking back, I was odd in many ways. I carried an urn during high school, and kept candy in the urn. Going to a small high school, this raised more than a few eyebrows. Now, years later, it seems I have become a legend of sorts for my alma mater.

*

SHARON GEE-MASCARELLO
Sharon is a 53-year-old funeral director and embalming instructor in the Mortuary Science Program at Wayne State University in Detroit

I remember standing before my aunt's casket. Instead of experiencing feelings of loss and mourning, I was uneasy and fixated on the odd and lumpy appearance of her face. I knew that she had been struck by a car, but I didn't expect her face to look like it had been struck by a car! I realize now that my young self was unimpressed with the facial restoration work. In mortuary school, I recalled that same visual experience so many times that it became a personal motivation during restorative arts class. While I had yet to learn the methods for successful restoration, I understood very well those that didn't work.

At the time of my aunt's funeral, I was unaware that I would embrace a career in funeral service. I do remember my mother being very supportive of my decision. I recall her saying, "Honey, I hope you will do better work on people who have been in accidents." I have also gained the wisdom to withhold judgment upon the work of others, not knowing the initial embalming analysis. Every professional embalmer strives to improve the condition of the decedent within their care. I am grateful to my aunt for teaching me this lesson.

*

LOUISE GOHMANN
Louise is a 61-year-old mortuary school educator
and funeral director in Jeffersonville, Indiana

Throughout my life, I avoided funerals and funeral homes at all costs. If I had to go to a funeral home, I slipped in, signed my name in the registration book, and slipped out as fast as possible. This was ironic because our neighborhood is right next to a cemetery. I walked there often, and taught my children how to drive in that cemetery! But when it came to funerals, I was known as "she who would not go."

So it came as no small shock to my family when I went to work for a cemetery and funeral home combination. I had been working as sales manager for a fundraising company, and was thoroughly miserable. One day, the funeral home ran an ad in the local paper looking for a salesperson. Imagine how desperate you must be to leave a secure job and jump into a commission-only position at the place you dreaded the most!

My job became selling cemetery plots, mausoleums, and prepaid funerals. I spent hours "standing funerals" at graveside services, acting as pallbearer, and meeting people to help plan funerals, choose a grave and create a memorial. The standard line that any funeral or cemetery salesperson says is, "I help people on the worst day of their lives." But what I discovered about myself is that I love to help people. It was at my lowest point that I took the job, but before too long I discovered I had a passion for easing the steps of families grieving for loved ones.

*

KAREN JELLY
Karen is a 44-year-old funeral director
and mortician in Havre, Montana

I began working for a funeral home as the office manager in 2001, as I held a degree in business, and they needed the help. At first, it was not really any different than any other business position I had held. The state I lived in at the time did not require a license for funeral directing, and, as we became very busy, our mortician trained me in funeral directing so I could help him out with those duties.

I really didn't think funeral directing would be any different than anything I had done before, but I was so wrong. And I was hooked. The satisfaction of a job well done, and the emotional reward when I was able to help a grieving family really touched me. As we continued to work together, the mortician would occasionally tell me I needed to get my mortuary science degree because I "was a natural." I honestly thought he was nuts. I had absolutely hated biology in high school, and that class would be child's play compared to the anatomy and physiology classes I would have to take just to enroll in the mortuary science program.

Over the next couple of years, I wrestled with the idea of attending mortuary school. In 2004, I made the decision to obtain the remaining prerequisites to attend. Around the time I was accepted into the program, my first marriage ended. School, work, and my children were my mainstays. Here I was, a thirty-four-year-old single mother, going back to school. It was frightening and exhilarating. I did have the full emotional support of my parents, who lived about 1,100 miles from me, as they indicated that I was always meant to help people. Amazingly enough, my children were not upset with my decision, and they encouraged me to go forward with it.

*

CODY JONES
Cody is a 37-year-old progressive funeral home owner
and funeral director in Bryan-College Station, Texas

I played hide-and-seek in the funeral home as a kid but I never planned on working in it. It wasn't until my dad died from leukemia when I was twenty-four that I first contemplated mortuary school. As a family business I did appreciate that I was never pressured into the profession, but found it in my own way in my own time. When Dad died, I moved from California back to Texas, to be with my mother and assist my grandfather who had to come out of retirement when my dad passed away. It wasn't an immediate decision to stick around, but as time passed it was apparent I had a skill for connecting with families and earning their trust. Eventually I made the commitment to continue as a fifth-generation funeral director and owner.

*

CORIANN MARTIN
Coriann is a 42-year-old funeral director
and embalmer in Kenosha, Wisconsin

My decision to enter funeral service came to me in high school. It wasn't necessarily an immediate decision, it was more intriguing than anything. Influenced by my favorite teacher, he sparked an interest in a career that seemed like a good fit. I wasn't necessarily one hundred percent sure this was my destiny but my personality is one that when I know I want something, I go for it, wholeheartedly. My family was very supportive and love telling people what I do. I think they get a kick out of seeing people's reaction!

*

JENNIFER PARKS
Jennifer is a 45-year-old certified funeral
celebrant in Santa Barbara, California

I was six weeks postpartum. I had newborn twins and a four-year-old at home. My hormones and emotions were all over the place. My best friend's parents owned the mortuary at the time and I had just left my previous employment prior to delivering my babies. My best friend's mom asked me to come work for her. I said, "No, thank you."

She said, "You will be great at this, we will train you."

I replied, "No way! I will cry all day long!"

But eventually I relented and the rest is, as they say, history.

My background was in women's healthcare helping to deliver babies, and it was a baby who brought me into helping families at the end of a life. I never in a million years would have thought that I would do this work. I can honestly say that it chose me and I couldn't imagine doing anything else.

*

LACY ROBINSON
Lacy is a 38-year-old Director of Member Development for the
National Funeral Directors Association in Brookfield, Wisconsin

I was in the eighth grade when my grandfather died. Eight months later my other grandfather died. I remember every detail about both funerals like it was yesterday. My interest in funeral service began during that time. When I started working for the local funeral home four years later I knew I wanted to pursue a career in funeral service. For me it had a nice mix—always something interesting happening, new information to learn and helping families in a meaningful way.

*

SHAWNA RODABAUGH
Shawna is a 37-year-old funeral director and
embalmer in Mount Pleasant, Michigan

When I was in elementary school, I lost a dear friend to natural causes. The impact of her funeral stuck with me, and it was ultimately what made me decide to enter the industry. As I got older, my intense desire to help people and interest in the science of preparation further fueled my resolve, and I decided to dedicate my life to funeral service.

*

STEVE TWEEDLE
Steve is a 42-year-old funeral
director in Ocala, Florida

For me, it took a while to come to the realization. I mostly took the job because it was a full-time position that was flexible around my college schedule. After working at the funeral home for a while, I realized what it meant to be a funeral director. I saw the care they gave to families, and the care they took when they handled people who had died. I started working full-time at the funeral home when I was nineteen. It was one of those moments in life when you realize things are changing and you're seeing the bigger world.

When I started talking to my family about how I was feeling, they were a little apprehensive. I was a quiet, shy person and all they knew of funeral directors was the guy who hired me. He's the exact opposite. They weren't sure that it was a wise career choice for me.

*

BRIAN VAN HECK
Brian is a 41-year-old funeral director in
the Lake Norman area of North Carolina

Seeds of interest in funeral service were planted in my young impressionable mind at the age of seven when my parents and I cared for an elderly neighbor. The seeds continued to grow throughout my elementary years in Catholic school, but it wasn't until I began working part-time in a funeral home during graduate school that my passion for funeral service blossomed.

There wasn't a huge disconnect from my educational endeavor and funeral service as I was pursuing a master's degree in counseling with a specialty and area of interest in death, dying, bereavement and end-of-life concerns.

Once I began working in the funeral home I could not get enough. I would come to class in the traditional funeral director attire (dark suit, white shirt and conservative tie) either because I had just come from work at the funeral home or was heading there right after class. I truly loved the environment and work of the funeral home setting. I was blessed with some fabulous mentors who taught me a great deal and for them I am grateful and owe much of what I have been able to achieve in my career.

At one point I considered leaving the pursuit of my master's degree to attend mortuary school in order to become a funeral director because I loved the work so much. At the advice of my educational mentors however, I completed that degree and went on to a doctoral program in counseling psychology.

I could not let go of the passion that I had for funeral service and found a funeral home to live in and work at while pursuing my Ph.D. After two years of coursework in that academic crusade, I realized I had no idea what I wanted to do with that degree once I earned it. With several major hurdles ahead of me in order to earn the title of doctor, I took a leave of absence from the program and went back to work at the funeral home where it all started. After a few short months, I knew that funeral service was, and is, my professional home. While my path was not the most direct to eventually earning the license and title of funeral director, the journey was most rewarding and I would not trade it or have had it designed any other way.

*

KIMBERLY VARELA
Kimberly is a 41-year-old funeral director
and embalmer in Westland, Michigan

I knew in my late teens. I loved science, especially when it did not include math. I had a knack for learning organ systems and functions. My mother, like most mothers, was convinced I would be a doctor. I was hoping to become a veterinarian. Ultimately, both well-wished careers were not all showbiz made them out to be.

I was turned on to the mortuary science program by a friend in college, but fate handed me a fifteen-year delay on my student debt by landing me a job in airfreight logistics. It came full circle after that career dried up, and I knew my love for the funeral industry hadn't changed. I loved what I could do for my families and for the deceased. There was no doubt I had found my niche.

*

DAN WELCH
Dan is a 30-year-old funeral director and
embalmer in Wichita, Kansas

The night I felt the calling that so many funeral directors speak of took place in February 2010. It's a night I've played through my head thousands of times, and will never forget. It is the night I remind myself of when I'm feeling worn out with funeral service, or when a death call comes in at 3:30 in the morning. That night changed my life's path.

I sat alone working the door at the funeral home that evening for nearly three hours without a single person crossing the threshold. We had two bodies lying in state and both of them had scheduled visitation times for the next day, however it was customary at this firm to stay open until 8 p.m. every night if a body was ready for viewing in the off-chance that the family may want to come by. That off-chance happened to me that evening.

About five minutes before I was to close, a lady in her mid-thirties came walking through the door. I did not recognize her but she quickly introduced herself as Damion's mother. My heart stopped because I knew that Damion was the nine-year-old who was killed in the house fire days earlier and was one of the decedents lying in state. Here standing before me was a grieving mother coming in to see her deceased son for the first time—by herself.

I offered my condolences to her and politely offered to take her to the room where Damion was lying in state. As we walked down the hallway she began to softly cry. As we got to the door I slowly opened it and told her to take as much time as she needed. Our eyes locked for just a moment before she cried out, "Please go in there with me!" Without a moment of hesitation I put my arms around her and assured her I would be by her side.

Unfortunately, we never made it completely into the room that night. As the door opened the remainder of the way, she caught a glimpse of her son for the first time lying in the casket some twenty feet inside the room. For the next hour and a half I stood there with a stranger, holding her in a tight hug as she wailed. It was a cry I will never forget—a deep, guttural moan that only a person who has lost a child will probably ever fully understand. It was a cry that I have never heard since that night, and honestly, a cry I hope I never hear again.

But that cry, that moment, was when I finally knew that funeral service was my calling—the one true ministry I could offer to people when they were in their deepest of valleys. Standing behind a pulpit was no longer viewed as ministry to me. Holding and helping people after a loss, that was my new ministry.

*

CHAPTER THREE

The Passion to Serve

The goal is to work toward a world where expectations are not set by the stereotypes that hold us back, but by our personal passion, talents and interests. -SHERYL SANDBERG

Driven by a passion to serve someone in their time of need, the daily duties of funeral staff include a hidden myriad of elements that are poignant and heartwarming. What do you love most about your job?

*

STEPHEN BARON
Stephen is a 64-year-old funeral service
licensee in Grand Haven, Michigan

I would have to say there actually are two real loves that I have in my job. First, for the most part, I love the people I meet whether they are whole or broken. We all get our chance at being both. Second, I enjoy opportunities to help make order out of chaos. Working with the brokenhearted is not always an easy task, but it is very gratifying to help people take the first steps toward adjustment and acceptance.

*

CHASTIN BRINKLEY
Chastin is a 47-year-old funeral director, embalmer
and cremation specialist in Buckley, Washington

The Peace Corps has the best motto, "The toughest job you'll ever love." I love my job and there are not a lot of people who can do it or who are willing to do it. I look forward to the moment of peace when family members first view a person who has died as a result of a traumatic or prolonged and wasting illness. Much technical skill and time goes into preparing a person for viewing. The positive psychological impact of someone seeing a loved one at peace is great. To see and hear the relief come over the survivors is rewarding for me as I realize the great gift I have given them.

*

JENNI BRYANT
Jenni is a 41-year-old funeral director
and embalmer in Maryville, Tennessee

The thing I love the most about my job are the people I meet and am able to help. I feel like I am able to help people at the worst time in their lives. I am able to give support and guidance to help them plan a meaningful celebration of life service. I love to hear their stories also. Everyone has a story to tell about their loved one who died. Sometimes those stories are not happy stories, and other times they have amazing stories of their life and even the care leading to their death.

*

LAUREN BUDROW
Lauren is a 44-year-old funeral director
and funeral service educator

What I loved about my job at the funeral home was the variety of personalities and experiences I was exposed to. I never knew from one day to the next what type of situation I might be making arrangements for, the family dynamics that might be present around the table, and the kind of ceremony I would be helping to facilitate. My days were filled with interesting events and people because I was working at a firm where each director was meeting well over one hundred calls each. My colleagues and I were constantly moving from one service to the next.

The other thing I loved about my job was my colleagues and the vendors. Once you are in funeral service, any aspect of it, you bond immediately with a fraternity of practitioners who are compassionate and want to help. I relied on my colleagues in order to put together and take care of the families I was serving. I have never felt that comfortable around any other group of people.

*

JASON RYAN ENGLER
Jason is a 36-year-old funeral director, certified celebrant,
and cremation historian in Rogers, Arkansas

I cannot even put into words the personal satisfaction that comes with taking care of people in their times of need. I am certain that many have preconceived notions of what a funeral director is, but for me being a funeral director represents the ability to honor the lives and the memories of those who have lived and loved and died. In caring for the dead and the living that survive them, I truly feel that we have one of the most sacred duties of any profession. When someone dies, whether unknown or of renown, someone is affected by the death. Whether it is on an individual, a community or even on a larger level, the fact that we are allowed into the lives of those who have entrusted their dearest loved ones to us is a privilege and an honor. I can't put this any other way.

*

SHARON GEE-MASCARELLO
Sharon is a 53-year-old funeral director and embalming instructor in the Mortuary Science Program at Wayne State University in Detroit

I enjoy challenge, and sought a vocation to challenge me. I love my work. I feel that caring for the dead and ultimately for the grieving is humanity's highest honor. I respect my vocation by refreshing my oath to serve others before every funeral, every arrangement conference, every embalming, every time, for everyone. This is challenging. Human nature favors the path of least resistance. I challenge myself to choose the high road.

I never want to think that it's just another funeral, just another dead body, just another day at work. I love what I do because it matters to the people I'm doing it for. Everyone deserves my best effort. I challenge myself to remember that.

*

LOUISE GOHMANN
Louise is a 61-year-old mortuary school educator
and funeral director in Jeffersonville, Indiana

I love the interaction I have with people. The individuals who want to celebrate a life with an all-out party, people who are brokenhearted, bewildered, or just plain angry at their loved one for leaving them. Sometimes their grief can be so heavy, but I try to show them that I can help shoulder some of the burden. I often say, "Your mother is now my mother, your child is my child. I will care for her as I would my own."

*

KAREN JELLY
Karen is a 44-year-old funeral director
and mortician in Havre, Montana

I've always loved to help people. Now I'm in a career where I can to do that each day. Whether it takes the form of background work such as setting up for services, drafting an obituary, dressing and applying cosmetics to their loved one, or assisting at the service, I know I am helping them. When I am the funeral director, I love taking an abstract idea of what families want and making it a reality, from the service folder to the music to the graveside. Families receive a great deal of comfort in following their loved one's final wishes, and helping them achieve that gives me great personal satisfaction. I also love working with people who feel the same way. Our funeral home is focused on the services we offer to families, and personalizing those services. It's wonderful working for a firm that focuses on the family.

*

CODY JONES
Cody is a 37-year-old progressive funeral home owner
and funeral director in Bryan-College Station, Texas

There are many aspects that I love about my job. Of course, as any genuine funeral director might enjoy learning about the deceased and their family, I appreciate the interactions with guests during visitations and funerals. However, I especially love receiving thank you cards from the families we serve. When families take time out of their busy lives to thank us, that is when we know we have really made a difference in their lives. Receiving a handwritten thank you definitely makes all the countless long hours and attention to detail really worth it.

*

CORIANN MARTIN
Coriann is a 42-year-old funeral director
and embalmer in Kenosha, Wisconsin

The favorite part of my job is educating people. I don't mean teaching; I mean explaining what we do, why we do it and showing them that death isn't so scary. Coming into a funeral home is very intimidating. People are often defensive and concerned about being taken advantage of. I love being able to sit with families and explain the process of planning a funeral. My goal is to always have a family leave knowing that I was honest, straightforward, and that I had their best interest at heart, not cost. I want more than anything for them to have a good experience. We have one chance to celebrate the life of their loved one, and I want to do my very best to make that happen.

*

JENNIFER PARKS
Jennifer is a 45-year-old certified funeral
celebrant in Santa Barbara, California

I love taking care of people. I love sitting with families and hearing their story. I love preparing for a funeral service, making sure all the details are tended to, and that their story has been told. I love the depth of emotion, the realness and rawness. This is what matters most. All of the superfluous nonsense of life has been stripped away and what is left is real, and then the healing can begin. I love being a bridge to that healing. I love bearing witness to the transformation that happens when we are allowed to truly grieve. Not skimming along the surface of life, but really getting down to the awful, ugly place where grief lives and then assisting people back to a place of wholeness and gratitude.

I also love tending to the deceased and using the talents that have been gifted to me to make someone's loved one whole again. To allow family members to see their loved one and be comforted by their body at rest. And finally, I love ancient rituals. Be they cultural or religious, they bring comfort because there is comfort in the familiar.

*

LACY ROBINSON
Lacy is a 38-year-old Director of Member Development for the
National Funeral Directors Association in Brookfield, Wisconsin

Since 2005, I've been serving the profession in the capacity of learning and development. I travel the country conducting customer service training programs for funeral directors and speaking at funeral conventions and conferences. I'm often asked if I had planned this part of my career after receiving my funeral director and embalmer license, and to be honest it was not on my radar.

When I was a student at Mid-America College of Funeral Service, we took a tour of Aurora Casket Company. I left there blown away by the manufacturing process and all the hard work that goes into making caskets. I was most impressed with the number of years employees had worked there. One lady in particular, Dottie, had been tufting casket interiors for over thirty-five years. Since that day, I've kept Aurora in the back of my mind.

At the time, my dad had great advice for me: earn my funeral director and embalmer's license, and learn as much as I could about working in a funeral home. He believed that experience would be invaluable to a supplier when I was ready to move on. When I made the transition to Aurora, I had an open mind about my future. I remember when JoAnn Baldwin, Aurora's manager of professional development, approached me about training. I thought, "Well, that sounds like fun. Why not give it a try?" I certainly had my early challenges but quickly realized helping funeral directors explore new ideas and improve their customer skills was energizing and fulfilling.

*

SHAWNA RODABAUGH
Shawna is a 37-year-old funeral director and
embalmer in Mount Pleasant, Michigan

My position is a little different than most funeral directors, in that I work with anatomical donation, and advocate and care for those donors while they are at our medical school. Future doctors, physician assistants and physical therapists learn from these donors, but what I love is speaking to them about the impact these donors have made on them. The intense gratitude of these students, and the care in which they treat the donors is the most rewarding thing.

*

STEVE TWEEDLE
Steve is a 42-year-old funeral
director in Ocala, Florida

There isn't an aspect of the job that I don't love. Every day I get to meet new people. The most important thing for me is helping people. I've helped people from every walk of life. I've been there for people I know, and people I don't know. Being the person who is there to help someone, especially when their world is falling apart, is very fulfilling.

It's good to know when I go home at night that I have done some good. I can't fix what has happened to a family, I can only try to bring some comfort to them. When I meet with the family, I spend a lot of time sitting with them learning about the person who has died. This is one of the things that I love the most. Getting to hear family stories, listening to the families laugh about something funny that happened.

This is when the healing begins, when we start planning the service, coming up with ideas for the service, to show and to celebrate the life that was lived.

*

BRIAN VAN HECK
Brian is a 41-year-old funeral director in
the Lake Norman area of North Carolina

The love of my profession and career in funeral service has and continues to evolve. In the early years, the love of learning this whole new unique and unusual world of funeral service and caring for the dead and the bereaved was fascinating. There was terminology, language to use, social and technical skills, and greater still was the learning of people and human nature to navigate through.

Before working in and around funeral homes, I often stated if I could get paid to people watch that would be incredible. In a sense, good funeral directing is people watching. As I watch people, whether it is the bereaved family or the friends and coworkers who attend a visitation, funeral or memorial service as guests of the family, I learn so much about people, community, society and culture. As human beings, we were created to be in relationship with others and to love one another. The call to funeral service that I have chosen to answer has allowed me to be in relationship with thousands of people and to offer a loving hand; I call that hand funeral directing.

So, in a word what do I love about my job? People. The greatest reward is receiving a hug from the family members upon conclusion of the service for their loved one and the words, "Thank you." In those moments it is like the whisper of God saying, "Well done, good and faithful servant."

*

KIMBERLY VARELA

Kimberly is a 41-year-old funeral director
and embalmer in Westland, Michigan

It may sound strange but I enjoy embalming. I am a voice for the deceased, and I like them to tell me their story as well. Whether it's a ninety-eight-year-old war veteran who passed peacefully surrounded by generations of his family, or a twenty-two-year-old heroin addict who died in an abandoned home, everyone is given the same respect. They all had someone who loved them and if they don't now, well I'm there to care for them. Bringing them back to a vision of their living selves is not something anyone can walk off the street and do. I feel a sense of maternal protection. I call the deceased by their names. Sometimes I even talk or sing along to the radio, as much to myself as to them. I'm told I have a knack for what I do. I know I have the heart for it.

*

DAN WELCH

Dan is a 30-year-old funeral director and
embalmer in Wichita, Kansas

There are many aspects of being a funeral director and embalmer that I absolutely love, however there are three that stand out above the rest.

The first aspect I love is having the opportunity to work with people. I know this sounds cliché, because you can work with people anywhere. However, I've found that the funeral industry is one of the few professions where you get the opportunity to work with the entire population regardless of socioeconomic status, race, sex, religion, and so on. In my five short years, I'm astonished by the amount of people I've had the opportunity to meet—and I've found that for every governor, ambassador, senator, television personality or famous athlete I've met, there are so many more homemakers, machinists, truck drivers, and farmers who have life stories just as unique. People are by far the number one aspect I love most about my job.

The second aspect I love is the feeling of satisfaction I get from helping families. I don't think there is a funeral director out there who does not enjoy that hug the family gives at the graveside. Even the most difficult families—the ones who make me pull out my hair—for some reason, when they give me that hug and say thank you, it makes it all worth it. I love pleasing people and helping them during their loss, and more often than not I find that their continual satisfaction is what brings me back to work every day.

The final aspect I love is embalming. I love to embalm. When I have the opportunity to embalm, I get excited. I love seeing the changes that take place. I love the chemistry and anatomy surrounding the embalming process. I love the challenge of taking a body that has been emaciated and eaten away by disease and restore it back to a state that a family will be pleased to see. I love embalming. I love my job.

CHAPTER FOUR

What Surprises Us Most

Let's not be afraid to receive each day's surprise, whether it comes to us as sorrow or as joy. It will open a new place in our hearts, a place where we can welcome new friends and celebrate more fully our shared humanity. -HENRI NOUWEN

Although being a funeral director is a profession born from caregiving, it also requires a strong skillset in many areas; a master multitasker who readily adapts to versatility at a moment's notice. Since choosing such a demanding career, what has surprised you the most about your job? What has surprised you the most about the profession?

*

STEPHEN BARON
Stephen is a 64-year-old funeral service
licensee in Grand Haven, Michigan

In spite of the irregular unpredictable hours involved in this work, there is usually time for the other activities that life brings. I admit that learning to relax and be flexible has not always been one of my strongest points, but if colleagues and family take care of each other, schedules can and do work to everyone's benefit.

Careers in any field require times of self-renewal and continuing education. These opportunities for professional and self-growth not only benefit the individual, but can and should result in great gains for the funeral service establishment the individual is associated with. Be they an owner or associate. I regret to say that after a lifetime in funeral service, I have known many more owner-practitioners who are able to give eloquent verbal statements on why associates are not to be valued in this way, than individual colleagues who understand that all licensees need and deserve continued growth opportunities.

Thankfully, through the educational requirements of many state boards, we are seeing a change in this attitude. In the past it would have been much more professional had funeral home owners valued good employees. Many did. Many did not. We've lost far too many good professionals due to simply not putting the gas in their tank so they could continue their good work. The biggest surprise for me has been the neglect of our own professional advancement.

However, on the plus side of the issue are the many new opportunities for continuing education that are offered today. These opportunities are offered by educational institutions, professional organizations and suppliers. The old cloak of secrecy that once seemed to surround funeral service has been replaced by openness and willingness to work closely with all other professions that provide services for the grieving.

*

CHASTIN BRINKLEY
Chastin is a 47-year-old funeral director, embalmer
and cremation specialist in Buckley, Washington

What is surprising to me is how people are moving away from visitations (viewings) and funerals. People are not willing to go through the process of grief. They want to skip the emotions and expense but want the benefit of having a funeral. They are talked into simply remembering him or her as they were in life, and funeral directors go along with it! We know better. We professionals should educate those we serve on the value of viewing and a meaningful funeral.

Nobody wants to go to the dentist to get a root canal. They are painful and expensive but you feel so much better when the dentist is finished. Funerals, like root canals, can be painful and costly. If a funeral director helps plan, coordinate and execute a meaningful funeral, the survivors will feel so much better.

*

JENNI BRYANT
Jenni is a 41-year-old funeral director
and embalmer in Maryville, Tennessee

The thing that has surprised me the most about my job is the willingness of people to help. When a death occurs, there are people who are willing and eager to go above and beyond to help a family during a time of need. Now, not all have the best intentions of the family in mind, but the majority of people do! I think the same goes for the funeral profession itself. Other funeral directors are always willing to help out a colleague. For instance, we once helped a family who lost four children in a house fire. The community rallied around this family to help them with whatever their needs were at the time. A local men's clothing store donated a suit for the father to wear since all of his clothes had burned in the fire. People donated furniture, food, money, and many other things. The funeral plans were for all four children to be buried at the same time and a procession was to go to the cemetery from the funeral home. At the time, we only had three hearses. A local funeral home called and wanted to help us out by lending us one of their hearses so the family could have the service the way they wanted. People are always willing to help!

*

LAUREN BUDROW
Lauren is a 44-year-old funeral director
and funeral service educator

What surprises me now about the funeral profession more than it did when I started is one, the way families are starting to shy away from having any contact with the deceased after death has occurred, and two, the rise of imported products within the American death care industry. There is such a shift on what families are willing to pay for their loved ones' services versus what they are willing to pay for themselves in order to "celebrate" afterward. The funeral has always been a celebration of life and funeral directors have been event planners for generations, we just didn't refer to either in those ways.

Now, the celebration doesn't need to have the deceased present at any point, and society is starting to try to eliminate the need for the funeral director as well. Respect for the profession has declined, and value toward the merchandise funeral homes sell has declined as well. The need for low-cost imports has become a necessity because of what families are willing to spend on the products that today seem to hold less importance than they once did. If society begins to hold less compassion for the dead, it will ultimately be detectable in how society chooses to take care of the living people around them every day.

*

JASON RYAN ENGLER
Jason is a 36-year-old funeral director, certified celebrant,
and cremation historian in Rogers, Arkansas

For me, the most surprising aspect of the funeral profession comes with the value we place on the importance of human remains and memorialization, especially with regard to cremation. I am often surprised at the number of families who ignore the necessity of permanent memorialization and its role in the grief process.

*

SHARON GEE-MASCARELLO
Sharon is a 53-year-old funeral director and embalming instructor
in the Mortuary Science Program at Wayne State University in Detroit

I am most surprised by the personal changes funeral service has elicited in me. I find that being a funeral director is self-actualizing. How I speak to a grieving family or a faith leader—the words I choose, how I deliver them, what my body language is telling—is vitally important to avoid misunderstandings or being perceived as disingenuous. I strive to be sincere in word and deed, free of pretense. In my personal life as well, I have gleaned the reward of paying attention to my inner voice and becoming more authentic.

*

LOUISE GOHMANN
Louise is a 61-year-old mortuary school educator
and funeral director in Jeffersonville, Indiana

People tell me all the time, "It takes a special person to do what you do," but I'm no more special than any other person who gets up and makes their way through every day. I feel privileged, but I get tired, cranky, and downright whiny sometimes, just like everyone else.

The thing that surprised me the most about my profession is that funeral directors and "death care" professionals have a wicked sense of humor. Not disrespectful, but along with the tragedy, we see the absurdity of life, and maybe as a defense, laugh longer and louder than others.

*

KAREN JELLY
Karen is a 44-year-old funeral director
and mortician in Havre, Montana

I think what has surprised me the most about my job is the changes we experience day to day. When I first came into the death care industry, services were pretty standard. Either they were burial or cremation. Now we have a blend of that, and keeping up with what the families want sure keeps me on my toes. Figuring out a way to provide what they want within the time frame they are looking at and legal constraints can be tricky, but I do my best.

What has surprised me most about the profession is the vast diversity of people in it. We have old-time morticians who've served families for forty years or more, some who have a difficult time with change. We have newer morticians who have served families for twenty years or more and are more acclimated to the idea of personalization. And we have new morticians coming out of mortuary schools with phenomenal ideas and technical skills who bring new life into an otherwise sober environment. All of us are striving to comfort and guide families who come to us in their time of need.

*

CODY JONES
Cody is a 37-year-old progressive funeral home owner
and funeral director in Bryan-College Station, Texas

Regarding our profession, I've been most surprised by how stuck in their ways the old-timers are. It took an act of congress to get my own grandfather to replace the carpet in our funeral home when I first started in 2004. Coming from a creative and technological background in my early twenties, I felt like I had turned an about-face. The funeral profession and the day-to-day processes seemed decades behind. It is amazing to me how long it has taken for our profession to understand that it needs to change just as our customers' needs and wants change. I don't know how to use a typewriter but we have one in our office!

*

CORIANN MARTIN
Coriann is a 42-year-old funeral director
and embalmer in Kenosha, Wisconsin

The most surprising part of my job is how so many families let you be a part of their family, if only for the few days that you work together. I have met so many wonderful people through the years and have kept in touch with many. I feel like the trust you build working so closely with a family helps create a bond that lets a family know that they can lean on you and that's what we're here for.

Although my job as a funeral director sounds morbid, I have been amazed at how much gratification there is. No two families are alike, no life story is the same and hearing the stories that families share just brings me that much closer to the realization that I picked the right career.

*

JENNIFER PARKS
Jennifer is a 45-year-old certified funeral
celebrant in Santa Barbara, California

I think I was surprised to find out how incredibly compassionate and empathetic the people in this profession are. I was told once that funeral directors have more empathy and compassion than hospice nurses and I believe it!

*

LACY ROBINSON
Lacy is a 38-year-old Director of Member Development for the
National Funeral Directors Association in Brookfield, Wisconsin

I transitioned to the National Funeral Directors Association in 2016. Serving as director of member development for the world's leading funeral service association is extremely rewarding. NFDA provides incredible training programs to assist funeral directors on their professional development journey. I am thrilled to be in a position to help funeral directors help families. I thrive on discovering new resources and tools to share with funeral directors.

Over the years I've had amazing mentors who have inspired and encouraged me every step of the way. I've met amazing funeral directors in this sacred profession who give one hundred percent every day. I carry with me their experiences alongside my own.

I often think back on the families I had the honor to serve. Their emotions have stayed with me and inspire me to continue on redefining what it means to honor a person's life.

*

SHAWNA RODABAUGH
Shawna is a 37-year-old funeral director and
embalmer in Mount Pleasant, Michigan

The most surprising part of my profession is learning my own stamina, and how much I don't mind the long hours when I think about why I work them. When I was working in traditional funeral homes, I knew that a call in the middle of the night meant that someone needed me. They didn't just need my services; they needed my comfort and my reassurance. My ability to provide that for them has been one of my greatest joys.

*

STEVE TWEEDLE
Steve is a 42-year-old funeral
director in Ocala, Florida

The amount of change in the industry is surprising. We are seeing more abbreviated services. It's a challenge to educate the public about how important it is to celebrate someone's life. That part is what really gets me excited about what I do. It's important to plan every service as an event, to celebrate the life with a unique experience during the service to show value in what funeral directors do. It's also the good side of being a funeral director. In general we have a bad reputation. Most people think of us as trying to rip people off, trying to sell a better casket to get more money. Any good funeral director doesn't care about that. They care about celebrating a life that was lived, making the service meaningful and unique.

*

BRIAN VAN HECK
Brian is a 41-year-old funeral director in
the Lake Norman area of North Carolina

As a death care provider, a large part of my work is helping individuals, families and communities create a meaningful ceremony that represents the life of their loved one who has died. It is not my place to critique or judge the ideas and decisions that they might have.

Rather, it is to direct, educate, guide and suggest ideas for how we can personalize the ceremony together, regardless of whether their choice is burial or cremation.

The most shocking and saddening aspect of my work is when a family elects to do nothing to commemorate, celebrate and honor the life lived. I believe that the death-denying culture and society we live in has fostered this decision that families make once death occurs. An example of this plays almost every time we go to a senior living community or assisted living care center to make the transfer of a deceased into our care. Upon arrival, the nursing staff will ask us to wait a few moments while they close all the doors so none of the other residents see. On one hand I understand a part of that. However, what about the opportunity for the friends to say goodbye to their friend and neighbor?

While we are a business and have to charge for what we do, the portrayal stories that make the evening news are the rip-off scams that funeral directors conduct and various ways that funeral directors take advantage of families. There is corruption, unethical and immoral conduct in our profession but the same rings true for clergy, physicians, lawyers and any other profession. Unfortunately the cameras quit rolling and news reporters are not around when we provide, at no charge, the funeral for the veteran or homeless individual or give of our time to do any number of community and charitable work; those stories don't sell or grasp viewer attention.

Interestingly, for as much of a death-denying world as our United States is, when a celebrity dies or tragedy occurs, the American public instantly becomes fascinated with death and funeral ceremonies. As I pen the words to this anthology, our country is grieving the loss of Muhammad Ali and trying to make sense of the death of forty-nine victims in a nightclub in Orlando, Florida, and five police officers in Dallas, Texas. The general public will watch hours of footage about death and stay glued to the television watching the families, celebrities and dignitaries commemorate, celebrate and honor the dead, but death in their neighborhood or own family is not treated the same and these are the very people with whom they are in relationship with. I believe that we all want to grieve death when it strikes our family, workplace or neighborhood but we do not know how. A good funeral director will and can assist, if only they would allow us to.

*

KIMBERLY VARELA
Kimberly is a 41-year-old funeral director
and embalmer in Westland, Michigan

In one word: bitterness. I am lucky that my family is small and close. I suppose I was raised in a naive bubble in that regard. I have watched families pull each other around by the hair over an insurance policy or some slight from long ago. I watched siblings who could not coexist in the same room at their parent's funeral. The level of anger, betrayal and hatred among some people toward each other does not cool at the death of a loved one.

I always think, or maybe more so hope, that those transgressions, real or imagined, can be put on hold until a loved one is laid to rest, but bitterness can run deep.

I see some of this same bitterness in this profession. One funeral director leaves a firm for a better job opportunity and suddenly their name is being dragged through the mud at every convention or meeting. Someone opens their own funeral home and you begin to hear whispers about how quickly it will fail or how incompetent the new owner is. I've most recently seen this in conversations on funeral director private Facebook groups when someone asks for help or guidance and within minutes the discussion turns ugly.

*

DAN WELCH
Dan is a 30-year-old funeral director and
embalmer in Wichita, Kansas

One thing that has surprised me about my job is the time commitment it takes to be a good funeral director. Over the years I have learned that there is no such thing as an eight-to-five funeral director. Being a great funeral director requires going above and beyond in all aspects to better please families. If that means coming to work early or staying late, then it must be done. This is likely the reason why the one thing that has surprised me the most about our entire profession is the overall laziness of some funeral directors across the country. It infuriates me when I read stories in the news about funeral homes cremating the wrong body or a funeral director cutting the legs off of a deceased because he forgot to order an oversized casket.

Laziness is also the likely reason behind the lack of professional improvement within the funeral profession. Although most states require their licensed funeral directors to have some sort of annual continuing education, it baffles me how flippantly most directors approach continuing education units. I feel CEUs are an opportunity for us as a profession to become better in every aspect. Unfortunately, the overall perception I have found is that continuing education is simply a burden to most and the majority of funeral directors who pursue CEUs are doing it to simply meet the minimum standard.

*

CHAPTER FIVE

The Biggest Challenges

Challenge is the pathway to engagement and
progress in our lives. -BRENDON BURCHARD

Every profession has unique challenges, and funeral directors are no
exception. Demanding schedules, missed family gatherings, and
compassion fatigue are common quandaries in the field dedicated to
handling our final rites of passage with the utmost delicacy. What is
the biggest challenge funeral directors face today?

*

STEPHEN BARON
Stephen is a 64-year-old funeral service
licensee in Grand Haven, Michigan

Today's funeral professionals face many challenges that our
predecessors never heard of, and didn't see coming. Challenges that
affect the way we practice to be sure, and challenges that govern our
business and operational methods. But it is those challenges that affect
the way we practice as individuals who've had the strongest influence.

Of those, it is my opinion that the change in the makeup, position and values of the family have caused the biggest challenges to funeral directors. These changes have in many cases, eroded the immediate support system which gave both purpose and value to much of the funeral process. In past generations, most uncles, aunts, cousins and grandparents lived within a day's ride of each other. The family gathered when life neared the end. Parents and grandparents came to live with their children when they were unable to care for themselves. When death occurred, the funeral was planned and usually accomplished with immediacy.

Today when funeral directors call families, they are often a continent away. Often you will hear in response, something like, "We visited Mom in the nursing home when we were in town last Christmas. She was not doing well. We all said our goodbyes during that visit. We would like you to do what is necessary to have her cremated and then please hold the ashes. Perhaps we will have a little service next August when we can all get to the family cottage."

Today I see us with more ways to stay close, yet we're separated more than ever. We push death and grief aside because it's not convenient. We live in an age when families are separated and people are lonesome. We live in a time when we need one another more, and yet we are often intentional about living apart. The funeral process is a process to begin the healing of wounds and pain left by loss. The big challenge for funeral service is to get people's attention long enough that we can get them to see the value in, and understand, the process.

*

CHASTIN BRINKLEY
Chastin is a 47-year-old funeral director, embalmer
and cremation specialist in Buckley, Washington

One of the biggest challenges facing funeral directors today is the ability to communicate the value of funerals to the families we serve. Funeral directors know how ceremony can help not only the family of the deceased, but the friends as well. I'm not talking about a funeral where the minister gets up to the podium and says, " I didn't know John, but I hear he was a great guy." As you get older and attend more funerals, you see a pattern—the same songs are sung, the same scriptures read. The only change is the name of the person who died.

I am not saying the traditional hymns or scriptures should not be used. I am just advocating for a service that is focused on celebrating the life of the individual who died. I am talking about a funeral where family members and friends are allowed and encouraged to participate in the ceremony, and to come up with ideas for the service as unique as the individual who died. In other words, we should not have the same funeral for Susie as we did for John. They are two different people who lived two different lives.

I admit that communicating our values is hard. We, as funeral directors, are selling a service that is not tangible. You cannot hold it or look at it before you buy it, or even take it home. You can only experience it.

*

JENNI BRYANT
Jenni is a 41-year-old funeral director
and embalmer in Maryville, Tennessee

I think the biggest challenge I face as a funeral director at this time in my career is making myself valuable to my employer. The death industry is changing. The cremation rate is continually going up, and people are looking elsewhere for their celebrations of life. Funerals have taken a turn away from what we call "traditional" to more of a celebration. Families want things that the funeral home didn't provide twenty years ago. I realize I need to be able to provide these things, and allow myself to think outside the box to keep these families at the funeral home.

I am very blessed to work for a company that realized this many years ago. They built separate buildings to accommodate families who don't want to be in the funeral home. We can accommodate everyone. We have an outdoor pavilion for less formal gatherings that include food and drinks. We also have two indoor buildings to use for memorial services. We, as funeral directors, have to either keep up with the changing trends, or get left behind.

*

LAUREN BUDROW
Lauren is a 44-year-old funeral director
and funeral service educator

The biggest challenge funeral directors face today is the public's understanding of the job that the profession undertakes. So often the role of today's funeral director gets lost in the cost of the services and merchandise, and what is most convenient for the family. Arrangements can now be made online and families can sign documents via fax or email and never see a funeral director or shake their hand.

American culture seems to be shying away from interacting with funeral service, and instead is treating it more like a death disposal service, negating the role of the licensee that is trained to assist the family. This has unintended consequences long term, however. The funeral profession evolved over time because families needed someone to assist them with the funeral details so they could focus on grieving. Removing the funeral director from the equation and thus opting for immediate dispositions without a service, families struggle to adapt to their loss.

*

JASON RYAN ENGLER
Jason is a 36-year-old funeral director, certified celebrant,
and cremation historian in Rogers, Arkansas

In my opinion, the biggest challenge funeral directors face is our reluctance to face change and adaptation. Families are changing constantly, and their desires and wishes are different than they have ever been. By and large, funeral directors have adapted to the growing wishes of families for personalization and unique funeral and memorial services, but they are getting more personal than ever before!

*

SHARON GEE-MASCARELLO
Sharon is a 53-year-old funeral director and embalming instructor
in the Mortuary Science Program at Wayne State University in Detroit

Change is constant. History repeats itself. Funeral service must flex in attitude and offering to maintain its relevance. Change is good. Rising to the ever-changing needs of the population and providing quality, reverent service to its deceased and grieving members builds a solid foundation. This bedrock is built upon, transformed, torn down and rebuilt again but core human values will repeat throughout history.

*

LOUISE GOHMANN
Louise is a 61-year-old mortuary school educator
and funeral director in Jeffersonville, Indiana

I am always amazed when someone says, "Funeral directors are rich, making all that money from funerals." Ours is a business, just like any other business. We have to keep the lights on, meet payroll, pay taxes, all while serving families at their most vulnerable. Our hearts war with our heads at times; we want to help people, but we have responsibilities to our own families, our employees, and our business.

We also have our own families who sacrifice having their spouse, mom or dad at their ball games, school plays, and anniversary and birthday parties. Unlike the movie, death never takes a holiday. Almost every funeral director I know has a story of leaving their home and family on Christmas to care for the deceased.

*

KAREN JELLY
Karen is a 44-year-old funeral director
and mortician in Havre, Montana

I believe that the biggest challenge funeral directors face, especially those who work in small funeral homes, is the challenge to balance our work and home lives. When we are working with a client family, it is as though they become our family, and because of that, our focus is on our client families. While we are at work, that is not a problem. When we get home, however, it is very difficult to change that focus, especially if the client families are calling in the evening or on the weekend, as we are trained to put the client families' needs above our own. When our children have a baseball game and a client has a visitation or vigil service, we have to be at work, thus causing disappointment for our children.

Because of the demands on our time and our attention, many marriages and families suffer because of our dedication to our work, and the families we serve. Some spouses and children are very understanding, but many times, the spouse, children, or both, feel as though they are second best or not important enough. We never feel this way. In many ways, how we serve our client families is the way we would want our family to be treated should the roles be reversed.

Unfortunately, this challenge has only worsened over time as, let's say forty years ago, in most households, only one parent worked outside the home, and the other was available to care for the children. This was the accepted norm. Now, in most households, both parents work, and the children become latchkey kids. The inability of one parent to consistently attend events causes further strain on the family dynamics.

*

CODY JONES
Cody is a 37-year-old progressive funeral home owner
and funeral director in Bryan-College Station, Texas

Funeral directors face many challenges. Among these challenges, we have to coordinate many family requests coming from different directions. In today's society, family members are more mobile and they are located all over the globe in different locations. Multiple family members are giving input and asking questions, and all these family members are connected through technology. Sometimes it's difficult to rein in all the demands and wants of family members in such a short amount of time without making errors, all while fulfilling their requests the best we can.

*

CORIANN MARTIN
Coriann is a 42-year-old funeral director
and embalmer in Kenosha, Wisconsin

I think the biggest challenge that funeral directors face is the ever-changing needs of our clientele. They want more experience-based services with themes and extravagant personalization. I love when a family wants something different and thinks outside the box of a typical funeral, but the challenge becomes finding the balance between celebration and dignity.

I have also found that integrating technology into funerals is getting more popular. Keeping up with cutting edge technology is something I find difficult because when you serve a customer base spanning over generations, you have to consider when technology is appropriate for a family or when they may consider it offensive. Having the technology available can be quite costly but you run the risk of falling behind the times and not staying competitive.

This also brings me to another topic of challenges that we face, which is how funeral homes can be so competitive. I've never been the competitive type but I see the way funeral homes compete for business and undercut competitors to get the client. Funeral homes are so critical and judgmental of other firms in the community. I would love to see that change. We all do this for the same reason. Accepting that not all funeral homes are the same, we need to acknowledge that we all fill a niche to meet the needs of caring for our deceased community.

*

LACY ROBINSON
Lacy is a 38-year-old Director of Member Development for the National Funeral Directors Association in Brookfield, Wisconsin

One of the biggest challenges we face is communicating the value of funeral service in a country where client families have more access than ever to reliable resources and perhaps a strong network of friends and family to assist in honoring their loved ones. Families may feel inclined to request minimum services from the funeral director, such as cremation with no services. It's the funeral director's responsibility to convey the value of planning a meaningful tribute, as well as how the funeral home can play an important role during this time.

There are several factors that have contributed to families making decisions and plans without a funeral director involved. I believe the biggest contributing factor has been the internet. Not only can families find similar merchandise items, but they also have the opportunity to read about new and interesting ideas for remembrance and gain the opinions of friends and family through social media. Families may also come across negative articles about unethical or criminal acts taking place in a funeral home. All of that combined, impacts the decision-making process for families and can present challenges during the arrangement conference for the funeral director.

It's important for the funeral director to believe in their heart that the service they provide to families is positive and special for everyone involved. When a funeral director can articulate to family why seeing their loved one is important and why they should consider planning a funeral, it changes the dynamics of the arrangement conference and ultimately their grief journey.

*

SHAWNA RODABAUGH
Shawna is a 37-year-old funeral director and
embalmer in Mount Pleasant, Michigan

I think one of the biggest challenges I've faced as a funeral director, is keeping my own emotions controlled in the face of a tragedy. Sometimes it can be difficult to remember that as hard as a situation might hit you, the people sitting in front of you, arranging a service, are dealing with one of the worst times in their life. They need your strength and composure to make it through the process, as well as your compassion.

*

STEVE TWEEDLE
Steve is a 42-year-old funeral
director in Ocala, Florida

The biggest challenges we face are trying to get people to understand that not all of us are bad apples. A vast majority of us are in it because we want to help. We are in this job because we were called to serve. Sure, there are a few bad funeral directors, just like there are bad bankers, bad car salesman, bad lawyers, and bad teachers. Our bad funeral directors are magnified because of the sensitivity of what we do. For every one bad funeral director you show me, I can give you ten who are productive members of the community. I can give you fathers who miss their son's soccer games or daughter's tennis matches because they are with someone else's family. I can give you funeral directors who are in civic organizations like Rotary and Kiwanis. I can give you more who volunteer at their churches and are deacons, or feeding the homeless at Thanksgiving. One bad funeral director who mistreats a family or loved one is on the 6 and 11 p.m. newscasts, while the good funeral director is hugging a widow or consoling a child whose father was killed. This is a difficult challenge to overcome, and we, as funeral directors, have to keep fighting the good fight. We have to remember that what we do is being watched every day by everyone. We have to remember that what we do is important and that it makes a difference.

Another big challenge is to help people understand how important services are. I always tell people you can't live on this earth for sixty, seventy, or eighty years and not impact someone's life. It's important to know that services are not to focus on the death that has occurred but on the life that was lived. It's important to take time out of your life, to slow down and to honor someone who has passed away, remember the time they were here, and reflect on what they meant to you. This challenge is an easy fix. It's important to listen to what every family is telling you. Our job is evolving from a profession that takes care of a dead body and facilitates a funeral. We are event planners; we are in the business of creating experiences. Every service should be planned with detail.

Too many funeral directors plan around the funeral. They plan where people will sit, where the pallbearers will stand, what music will be played, what time the minister will talk. They don't plan when a specific song will be played that they learned was important to the decedent and his wife. They don't plan the coffee toast with the decedent's favorite coffee (or other beverages). We need to find out if the decedent loved old cars and plan a car show the night of the visitation. If we don't start learning these things during the arrangement process and start planning them into the funeral, we will be extinct.

*

BRIAN VAN HECK
Brian is a 41-year-old funeral director in
the Lake Norman area of North Carolina

The educational journey that led me to discovering myself and the passion for funeral service that was inside me since boyhood, was not the most direct path to becoming a funeral director. However, I believe it made me a better funeral director and well-equipped to handle some of the challenges facing the profession today. Ironically, the challenge I would identify as most impactful today is education.

Having identified education as the challenge, I believe there are two aspects that create such a struggle for my profession. The first is the actual educational requirement for funeral director licensure. While there is a national board examination that must be taken and passed upon completion of the mortuary science program, each state has established their own educational requirements for licensure. The spectrum of education for obtaining a license ranges from high school diploma to a four-year bachelor's degree in just a very few states.

I fully recognize that education in itself will not make an individual a better funeral director. But it does make them more mature. It also provides additional time to develop certain skill sets that are vital to the profession, and gain more professional experience along the way. Across the country our profession has a great need for a higher number of qualified candidates coming out of school or with three to five years of experience. Creating more uniformity of our educational requirements can only help this challenge.

Today's funeral service family (customer) is much more educated and informed about options due in large part to the information available to all of us at our fingertips through our smartphone and internet. Like other professions, we have to combat the myths, misconceptions and untruths that might be posted by any number of bloggers or webmasters.

Over the last decade we have also seen a huge influx in the number of bereaved individuals who are price shopping either via phone or walking into a funeral home to obtain pricing information. As a result, the role of funeral director and funeral service professional has in large part become one of educator. I must now listen to the family and educate them on a plethora of options that they are not aware of because, while they are fifty or sixty years old, they have never before engaged in this process. It becomes a true case of they don't know what they don't know. Further, I represent and am talking to them about services and merchandise that they really do not want to select and purchase because someone they love is dead. A funeral director who has been better educated and trained will be able to counsel and guide this family in the decision that is best for them, and the most appropriate way to honor the life of their deceased loved one.

*

KIMBERLY VARELA
Kimberly is a 41-year-old funeral director
and embalmer in Westland, Michigan

Burnout! We are people with lives, families, hobbies and health requirements. The public and others in the industry are very negligent of our time and the work involved. We are held to such a high public standard and an equally high work standard. Don't get me wrong, no one lied to me about this being a nine-to-five job but twelve to sixteen hour days, five to seven days a week cannot be sustained for long. Funeral directors wear their timecards like badges of honor. "Look at how much I worked and have been for years. If you can't hack it then get out." There is no recourse. If you complain, you are weak. If you cannot be there, you feel that you let your family down. It's a fine line between being dedicated and being overworked.

*

DAN WELCH
Dan is a 30-year-old funeral director and
embalmer in Wichita, Kansas

I believe the number one challenge funeral directors face today is the ability to illustrate the importance behind the memorialization of a loved one. It is no mystery that cremation rates have been on the rise for many years here in the United States. However, in my short time as a funeral director, I have seen not just an increase in cremation, but even more concerning is an increase in families who have a direct cremation with no services. It astonishes me the number of people who walk into the funeral home and request the easiest and cheapest package. We've grown into a society that wants to move on as if nothing ever happens after death. It has become the funeral director's challenge to respectfully educate families on the necessity and importance behind having a service—without trying to appear as though we are upselling to families.

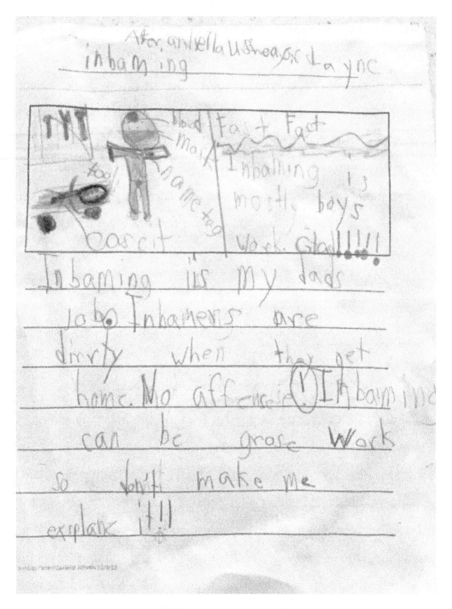

Artist: 7-year-old Layne Barz

CHAPTER SIX

The Emotional Impact

A life is not important except in the impact
it has on other lives. -JACKIE ROBINSON

Funeral staff do their best to shield us from the horrors of death, but they are human. Juggling their own emotions as they skillfully tend to duties can sometimes pose a challenge, even for industry veterans. What was the one death that really hit home for you?

*

STEPHEN BARON
Stephen is a 64-year-old funeral service
licensee in Grand Haven, Michigan

Most funeral directors could devote a chapter to answering this question alone. My father once said to me, "If you choose to practice the profession, you will experience that the deaths that will be the hardest for you, the ones that can take the most out of you, are the ones where the deceased is your age or younger. So the longer you practice, the more of yourself you invest." It took time for the truth of that statement to become clear.

When I was a young man and was an expectant father, I had all the hopes and fears of any man going through this joy. Admittedly, I was not considering any complications that would result in any type of bad outcome. The next time around, not being quite so naive, it was different. Maturity does that.

At the birth of my children, I was privileged to be present in the delivery room. What happened within hours or days of their birth was one of the greatest teaching moments I was ever part of. In a short period of time after the births of my children, I found myself answering the call of new parents who had lost their child in the birth process. One of the times occurred in the very hospital where our family was. We were celebrating the joy and wonder of birth. Others were confused, felt abandoned and had deep pain and sorrow. I remember so much about these deaths, but what I remember most was holding a lifeless child as I took them from the hospitals...and each time I remember rushing, as soon as time allowed, to make sure our babies were all right. An experience such as these can't help but raise questions in your mind and fill your own heart with Thanksgiving.

*

CHASTIN BRINKLEY
Chastin is a 47-year-old funeral director, embalmer
and cremation specialist in Buckley, Washington

In 1994, only being licensed a little more than a year and a half, I arranged my first double service. The funeral home received a call a few minutes before 5 p.m. from a family insisting on making funeral arrangements right away for their parents, who had just been murdered. Most of my coworkers wanted to go home and have supper with their families, so since I was single at the time, everyone seemed to look at me. I went to the family's home and was there for several hours. The family told me their parents owned and operated a small grocery store where they were murdered during a robbery. This couple's murder was tragic and became more evident as I was embalming their mother. She was shot in the face but the bullet went through her hand first. I kept envisioning her on her knees begging for her life. It was very heartbreaking. One night, over a decade later, I was on my computer and went to the newspaper's website in the city where this murder took place. A news article caught my eye where the state of Texas executed a man for a double homicide. As I read the article, it became evident who the paper was talking about. I thought to myself, "Justice was finally served."

Another service that bothered me was that of a borderline elderly woman. I embalmed her late one afternoon. She was beaten to death. She did not have more than one square inch on her body that was not bruised. I felt bad for her, imagining the pain she must have endured. This type of homicide is similar to victims of multiple stab wounds. The crime is usually perpetrated by someone with a close or intimate relationship with the victim. In this case, her relative was immediately arrested. The police later had to release him for lack of evidence and he attended the funeral. It was hard to look at him. I never heard if justice was served.

*

JENNI BRYANT
Jenni is a 41-year-old funeral director
and embalmer in Maryville, Tennessee

The death of a child is always hard. There are so many ways to describe it, but the word "hard" just sums it up for me. And I mean hard in every aspect, from the first call to the service. Every detail is hard. The plans I make and the phone call I make every single day to help a family, become totally different when I am making them because of the death of a child. I have had friends, people I have met a few times, and complete strangers lose a child. It is always hard!

There is one service that really stands out to me. There was a very tragic accident that resulted in the death of a nine-year-old boy. I met with his family and stayed with them every step of the way. I cried with them, laughed with them, and got mad with them. This family was young, they had never experienced a death and really needed my help. It is always great to be needed, but in this case, it is never good.

*

LAUREN BUDROW
Lauren is a 44-year-old funeral director
and funeral service educator

It is almost impossible to narrow down all my funeral services to the one most bothersome. Each service had something that touched or disturbed me in some way. There is one service that does stand out to me and it actually turned into two services. I buried a beautiful nine-month-old girl who died from a congenital condition that the family knew she would not survive. Nothing in mortuary school can prepare a new practitioner to see babies of any age in a tiny casket covered in a flower spray larger than the casket. The baby looked perfect with her red lips and bright orange hair. I was not prepared for the mother's reaction at the conclusion of the service though. As she went up to say her goodbye, she lay onto her baby and begged forgiveness for having given this illness to her. Of course this was not anything the mother had any control over, but her guilt was evident. What I did not know was the mother was carrying a second child at the time and was about five months along. This second baby girl was born with the same congenital condition and lived only five months. I buried both babies within a year with the same casket. Same flowers, same orange hair, same family, same guilt. It broke my heart.

*

JASON RYAN ENGLER
Jason is a 36-year-old funeral director, certified celebrant,
and cremation historian in Rogers, Arkansas

The death of my Granny, my grandmother, hit home for me. Deeply. Intensely. Personally. I spent my entire childhood as Granny's boy, and her death in February 2016, impacted me on a visceral level. It seems that we can spend our entire lives preparing for the death of someone we love, but when the time comes we can't be fully prepared.

Granny played such an instrumental part in my upbringing, and her death truly changed my life. At age eighty-five, in seemingly good health, she passed away unexpectedly after suffering a stroke and from injuries sustained from the subsequent fall.

The professionals at the funeral home we called on, many of whom I had known for years, made her passing more bearable for my family and for me, both personally and professionally. After a beautiful service of remembrance, Granny was cremated and her spirit set free. Her purified remains were lovingly placed in a MacKenzie urn, appropriately personalized, and interred by the hands of her loved ones in our family plot.

I have such a peaceful remembrance of the entire experience, even though going through the grief process was tumultuous. I've lost love, I've lost loved ones. But I couldn't have prepared myself for this loss, no matter how hard I might have tried.

*

SHARON GEE-MASCARELLO
Sharon is a 53-year-old funeral director and embalming instructor
in the Mortuary Science Program at Wayne State University in Detroit

Just yesterday I was pleasantly reminded of a long ago friend. So I searched her name and found the first entry of her obituary. I sat motionless for a very long time. She died four years ago without my own life skipping a beat.

*

LOUISE GOHMANN
Louise is a 61-year-old mortuary school educator
and funeral director in Jeffersonville, Indiana

The one death that really hit me hard occurred years ago. I met a woman who wanted to prearrange her funeral. She had cancer, and was facing a potentially disfiguring facial surgery.

I got to know her over a number of weeks, and regularly visited her at her apartment. She called often, asking me to come over because she wanted to make changes to her arrangements. She had been a June Taylor dancer in her younger years, and was still a beautiful woman, proud of her looks. We drank tea and leafed through her scrapbooks featuring pictures of herself with Bob Hope and other stars of the day. She was lonely and loved to tell stories, and I loved to hear them.

I discovered she had a love for horse racing. Because we live near Louisville, Kentucky, the Kentucky Derby was one of her favorite events. She would have enjoyed going to the track, but was too sick. I brought her a racing form so she could pick her horses for the big race, placed her bets for her, and told her I would bring the winnings to her the following week.

The date of her surgery loomed, and she was so afraid of what she would look like after. A few days before surgery, she called and asked me to come over right away. I explained that I was still at work, but would come in a few hours. She said, "You will get here before my daughter, right?" I told her I would get there as soon as I could. I called her daughter and said her mom had called, and I was going over in an hour to visit and make changes again. She said she was going to take dinner over about the same time. We arrived, along with a visitor from her church, and we all headed up to her apartment. On the door was a note: "Miss Lee, the door is unlocked, and my clothes are on the chair." We looked at each other. This lady was a New Yorker, and had no less than four locks on her door, which was always shut tight.

We went in and saw her lying on the couch, fully dressed, makeup and wig perfect, with a pillow on her chest and a blanket pulled up to her chin. She looked like she was sleeping but the gun on the floor told us otherwise. On a chair next to her were her dress, shoes, jewelry, the racing form, and the twenty-two dollars she owed me from the horse race. She could not face the idea of surgery marring her beauty, and did what she thought was the only thing she could do.

After the police and coroner left, her daughter said, "I can't believe my mother did this terrible thing to you. She set you up to find her. Why?" I told her that her mother loved her so much and wanted to protect her. "She trusted that I would find her and would know what to do to take care of her, and help you."

*

KAREN JELLY
Karen is a 44-year-old funeral director
and mortician in Havre, Montana

During my second year in my current location, I cared for an eleven-month-old who was beaten to death. My daughter was pregnant with my first grandchild at that time, and this little guy really affected me. I prepared him for his funeral, but really didn't want to give him back to be buried. His parents did not live together, and even though I realized that he would be going with the "safe" household, I was distraught, almost feeling like I could protect him.

In many ways, I grieved the loss of this precious boy and who he could have become.

Sometimes during times like this, especially with babies and toddlers, funeral directors can become attached to the child and don't want to let them go. It is the protective instinct present in all of us, wanting to protect them from further harm. I know it is irrational, but the feelings are there. I was truly fortunate in that I have strong support in my employer and my family, and that enables me to continue to care for those who cannot be protected.

*

CODY JONES
Cody is a 37-year-old progressive funeral home owner
and funeral director in Bryan-College Station, Texas

A good friend of mine passed away earlier this year from lung cancer at the age of thirty-seven. He left behind his wife and his young son. These types of unfortunate and unexpected deaths of our own friends and family make us shift back and forth between serving as funeral director and grieving as a family friend. He was a motorcycle enthusiast, so we rolled his bike right into our lobby next to the sign-in book. We really tried to honor him in a way that was most fitting. I wanted to make it extra special because he was a friend of mine, and that's what we want to do with every family.

*

CORIANN MARTIN
Coriann is a 42-year-old funeral director
and embalmer in Kenosha, Wisconsin

It's difficult to find the most memorable funeral I've ever had because there've been a number that stick out. The earliest funeral I remember that hit me hard was the death of a fourteen-year-old girl who committed suicide by way of a shotgun wound to the head. Her father was the one who found her and was understandably destroyed. The family was so devastated that they didn't want an open-casket viewing or to see her again. I try to always honor the wishes of the family but I had this overwhelming feeling that they needed to see her again. They finally agreed to allow us to try.

Through the funeral planning and days prior to her funeral, we did everything in our power to give this family a chance to see her again and hopefully keep the casket open for everyone to say their final goodbye. My goal was to be able to replace the last image the father had in his head of his daughter. We worked tirelessly for days and when the day of the funeral came, all I remember is the mother and father walking up the church aisle to see their daughter. A few minutes later the father came up to me and said, "Thank you so much for giving me my daughter back."

I saw an immediate physical shift in his body posture and facial expressions. I felt a sense of relief knowing that I gave that family the ability to remember her in her innocence and not in pain anymore. In that moment, I felt like I made a difference. I did what I set out to do, and although I felt like I had to push the parents to see her, I made the right call.

On a lighter note, one of the most memorable funerals that I arranged was for a man who had passed away while still legally married, although he had a long-time girlfriend. The arrangement conference was the first time these two women were going to meet. I'll be honest, I didn't know what to expect. Would this be a cordial meeting or should I prepare for the worst? The wife was very respectful and understanding because she knew that although they were still married, they were only married on paper. She told his girlfriend that she was only there for legal purposes and gave her free rein to plan the funeral as she saw fit. The meeting went well and they parted with a hug.

Fast forward to the funeral. The night of the visitation, the girlfriend approached me with a special request for the service the next day. Her boyfriend was a drag racing enthusiast and she wanted to know if we could make a pitstop on the way to the cemetery at the dragstrip. I was apprehensive because it had never been done before but she told me that she would arrange for the grounds to be open and would take care of contacting the necessary people to make it happen.

The next morning was by far, the most creative final goodbye I've seen. We drove in procession to the dragstrip and all pulled into the holding stalls. The girlfriend got into the hearse and I escorted all the guests into the stands. Our hearse driver drove the deceased down the dragstrip one last time! On the return pass, the entire crowd gave him a standing ovation. We returned to our cars and proceeded to the cemetery for burial.

It was an amazing tribute.

*

LACY ROBINSON
Lacy is a 38-year-old Director of Member Development for the
National Funeral Directors Association in Brookfield, Wisconsin

I'll never forget the death of a seventeen-year-old girl who was hit by a drunk driver. At the time, she and her twin brother had been enjoying a carefree summer before their senior year of high school. As a funeral director, there's this drive inside us that wants to help every family, but when it comes to helping a mother honor her child's life, you want to go to the ends of the earth to help, knowing that her pain will never go away. When you learn about a young person who had an incredibly bright future, was pure sunshine to everyone, and who was taken by such a senseless act, your heart breaks.

My goddaughter, Reagan Olivia Ferguson, died on June 2, 2006. She was just five and a half months old. Every day, family and friends had all hoped that Reagan would be one of millions of premature babies who make it home to live a healthy life. Watching my best friend Lauren and her husband Mark experience the birth and death of their first child changed the way I help grieving parents.

Lauren's strength when planning the funeral, and her desire to make Reagan's tribute special was inspiring. She always thinks of others, and wanted to make sure family and friends felt included. From the grandparents to the neonatal intensive care nurses, Lauren and Mark acknowledged their grief and showed deep appreciation for the acts of love. I learned invaluable lessons about helping young parents grieve that I carry with me to this day.

*

SHAWNA RODABAUGH
Shawna is a 37-year-old funeral director and
embalmer in Mount Pleasant, Michigan

After I gave birth to my son, the first family I cared for when I returned from maternity leave was a service for a baby who had passed in the bathtub. One of the most difficult things I've done was hold that baby and put her in the casket, knowing that my baby was safe and warm at home. The parents' grief was unimaginable.

As I sat with them in the viewing room, I picked the child up and allowed the parents to hold her one last time before guests arrived for the viewing. I will never forget the look on their faces as I placed her back in the casket, knowing that they'd never be able to hold her again.

*

STEVE TWEEDLE
Steve is a 42-year-old funeral
director in Ocala, Florida

Within a week or so of my son being born I got a phone call from the mother of a baby who died of SIDS, sudden infant death syndrome. As I was preparing for the family to come in, I realized the baby's last name sounded familiar. Then it occurred to me that I went to school with a student who died in high school. He was the brother of the baby's mother, making him the baby's uncle. I live in a fairly small community so the people we went to school with may not necessarily be the best of friends, but we all knew each other. As the family came in and I walked them back to the arrangement office, I told them I just had my first child. I said I wasn't sure what they were going to get from me, but I would do my best for them, and I would be devastated if I were them. The baby's grandfather was an imposing man, very gruff, huge in stature. He turned on me, got in my face, pointed his finger at me and said, "You will never understand what we're going through. You've never lost a grandchild AND a son!"

"You're right, I won't. But I want you to know that I went to school with your son. His death impacted all of us," I said.

He backed down and I think he realized that communities suffer along with families. During that arrangement we laughed and cried as we talked about their son and made arrangements for their grandchild. I can remember standing in the church putting the lid on the baby's casket. As we got ready to go to the cemetery, my tears dropped into the casket. This service really hit home with me on several levels. I learned that as funeral directors, people don't realize that we hurt. Death affects us too.

*

BRIAN VAN HECK
Brian is a 41-year-old funeral director in
the Lake Norman area of North Carolina

While I feel blessed and privileged to walk with each family while we arrange for a meaningful service for their loved one, there are two deaths and services that stand out in my career. The deaths of three-year-old Lance and two-year-old Brody happened almost exactly a year apart, and in a similar manner—drowning in the backyard pool.

Lance was the first tragedy. His father called and told me that his son had died and asked if they could come in and talk about some arrangements. He did not share any details regarding his son's age or circumstances surrounding the death in that initial phone call. We scheduled a time for them to come to the funeral home a short while later. Lance's parents came in and in a short period of time I learned that three-year-old Lance had gotten through the gate in the side yard that led to the backyard pool at the family's home while his mom went in to change the laundry. After getting through the gate, he made his way to the pool where he had played many times before. This time, however, he did not come out. Lance's physician parents were numb and in shock. They needed the listening ear and guidance of a funeral director, and God put me in their path to shepherd them through the loss of their precious son.

As we talked about how we were going to honor young Lance's life, his mom and dad told me they wanted to have Lance cremated because they wanted their little boy home with them as quickly as possible. They went on to tell me about the event they wanted at the funeral home to celebrate Lance's life and who he was. They shared with me that Lance's favorite color was lime-green. His favorite foods were bananas, grapes, popcorn and ice cream.

Over the next two days we converted the visitation room into Lance's room with over one hundred lime-green balloons, lime-green bowls with cut-up bananas and grapes, an ice cream sundae bar with all the fixings—donated from a local ice cream company—and a popcorn wagon in front of the funeral home. Additionally, for all of us working at the funeral home that day, I purchased bright lime-green neckties to wear in honor of Lance. At the end of the evening, the guests took a few moments to write messages to Lance on lime-green Post-It notes. They stuck the notes on the lime-green balloons and we walked outside to the front lawn of the funeral home and released them skyward to heaven and to Lance.

The following day I delivered leftover ice cream, snacks, flowers, and treats to the family home. Standing in the garage speaking with Lance's father, he said, "We have become very close this week, but you never mentioned if you have children or not." I told him that I did not. He looked at me and said words I will never forget: "You will make a great dad someday. I know, because of how you cared for my son."

In that moment, chills came over me and a simple handshake was too informal, so we embraced before leaving one another's company. As I drove back to the funeral home, I knew that I had served Lance's family well and honored the three years he was on this earth.

The second death occurred 350 days later. All the similarities between these two tragedies were unknown to me at the time. Again I received a call from a gentleman telling me that he needed to come in and talk about arrangements for his son who had died. After addressing a few questions over the phone, we set a time for him and any other family members to come in and start the arrangement process. A few short hours later, I was sitting across from a mother and father whose two-year-old son had drowned in the backyard pool less than twenty-four hours prior. Brody's parents showed me a picture of their little angel and told me that three days ago he had learned to go off the diving board in the deep end with his floaties on. Wednesday morning, he made his way to the backyard pool and went off the diving board by himself like he had done a few days prior. This time however, he forgot to put his floaties on and he didn't resurface. Firefighters and emergency medical service personnel tried to revive him, but Brody's young life was cut short.

During our time together over the next three days, it was my task to help this family begin to grieve well by honoring Brody's two years on this earth. I quickly learned that Brody's favorite color was blue, that he loved Mickey Mouse, Woody and Buzz Lightyear from Disney's Toy Story, Reese's Peanut Butter Cups and M&Ms, plain not peanut. As we continued to discuss the most appropriate way to celebrate and honor Brody's life, I planted the seeds in Brody's mom and dad that I wanted people to know who they were there to see when they walked into the funeral home. I encouraged them to bring in toys and things that represented Brody's life. We filled a suburban and two vans with all the memorabilia of this young life.

Let me tell you, when people walked into the funeral home and saw the abundance of blue balloons, Woody dolls, Buzz Lightyear, a multitude of other toys and stuffed animals, and the video tribute playing on the large drop-down screen, people knew we were honoring Brody. I also found four-foot Mickey Mouse and Buzz Lightyear balloons that we attached to the ends of his custom blue casket. The following day we gathered at the cemetery to lay Brody to rest and send love messages upward to Brody via blue balloons.

Both Lance and Brody's families created foundations to continue the memory of their sons. Lance's family set up a foundation related to rescued animals, while Brody's family established a foundation that has built playgrounds and ballfields, and provides scholarship money for children that cannot afford to play sports.

I will forever be connected to these two families. I see them around town from time to time and we always engage in conversation. While the interaction with me is a constant reminder of how and why our paths crossed, I can walk away knowing that those two boys were loved. When we love well, we grieve well. Together we all grieved the death of Lance and Brody. As humbly as possible, I say this: these families we well served, but I am grateful to God that not each and every encounter I have as a funeral director is due to the circumstances of a young child that died tragically.

*

KIMBERLY VARELA
Kimberly is a 41-year-old funeral director
and embalmer in Westland, Michigan

I had to embalm and prepare a young child. Mind you, I do not have children, but again I feel maternal to everyone in my care and this story was tragic. I had him in my care for close to a week while everything was arranged, and I dressed and laid him in his casket on the day of his visitation. I tried not to think about him but the court case involving the circumstances of his death was going on, and I would catch bits and pieces on the news. The little body lying on my table kept creeping back into my mind. It wasn't fair. I know death never is, but this one just kept rolling around in my brain.

On the day of the funeral I was tasked to meet the hearse at the crematory to remove the liner from the metal rental casket. Since there was so much room inside the casket, I wanted to take the body out first so he wouldn't bobble around as I separated the cremable liner from the metal shell. I placed my hands underneath the body and two crematory operators came to help me. My arms tightened around him and I barked at them to stay back. They were good friends of mine and I think they understood. I felt like he was my responsibility. He was small and fragile and I didn't want anyone else to touch him. I had taken care of him up to this point and I was going to be there the rest of the way. I wasn't going to leave him. The crematory was full of operators and everyone bowed their heads and clasped their hands as I carried his little frame, laid him on his pillow once more, and closed the container. You could hear a pin drop. It took me a while to come back from that but that child taught me a lot and I still remember his face as clear as day.

*

DAN WELCH
Dan is a 30-year-old funeral director and
embalmer in Wichita, Kansas

In 2013, my father was killed in a car accident. For seven agonizing weeks we did not know where my father was until we received a phone call that a hitchhiker found my father's car in a ravine. He had fallen asleep at the wheel and driven off the interstate where cars were unable to see him. I was blessed to have the opportunity to handle all the arrangements for my father.

Fast forward to 2015, I received a phone call from a man by the name of Steve. He informed me that his son had been missing for quite some time and the police had just recently found his body in an open field. I instantly felt a connection with this family and felt as though I needed to meet with them. Later that day they came in to make arrangements and explained how their son had gone missing. They began to express the sorrow and agony they had been experiencing while he was lost. It was as though they were reading my journal from when my father was missing.

After making the arrangements I went to our local coroner's office to take their son into my care to begin the preparation for viewing. As I unzipped the body bag, my knees went weak. The smell combined with the desquamation and putrefaction of human tissue instantaneously brought me back to the day I prepared my dad. There's not another funeral director or embalmer in this country that would have taken the amount of care and respect that I did for this boy. It was as though I was preparing my dad all over again. Every movement I made was dignified, methodical and intentional. I knew more about what this family was going through than probably any other person on the planet earth. I made it my personal goal to make sure they were happy.

While some of my coworkers suggested we keep the casket closed, I spent hours upon hours of my own time making sure this family could see their son. I knew what it was like to have someone tell me I shouldn't or couldn't see my dad—and I wasn't going to let that happen to this family. I knew the impact that viewing my father had on me in allowing me to move forward with my grief and I made it my personal goal to give that same opportunity to this family. To this day I still have frequent contact with this family and they have become dear friends, all because of a death that hit a little too close to home.

*

I HOLD THINGS

Kimberly Varela

You ask me what I do for a living.

"You work with the dead."

"You stand around, greeting people at the door."

"You answer the phone and file papers in a black suit."

All of these are true.

I am diverse.

I have many responsibilities.

Somedays I wish for the many arms of Kali

and her casual acceptance of death.

But you want an easy answer.

So here is the best answer I can offer.

I HOLD things.

I hold the hand of the widower when he questions what he will do without the love of his life at his side.

I hold the mother who cannot stand on her own after seeing her child in their casket.

I hold up the cemetery crew because the children need one more minute to say goodbye.

I hold back the crowd so a wife can have a moment of privacy with her husband.

I hold up my own plans with family and friends because loss calls at all hours.

I hold up my ethics to a standard befitting the deceased,

as if the walls were made of glass and everyone were watching.

What I do is not glamorous

But what I hold is precious.

I hold life and death in the span of hours.

I hold things until I know it is time to let go.

CHAPTER SEVEN

Fighting Fatigue

Public service must be more than doing a job efficiently and honestly. It must be a complete dedication to the people and to the nation.
-MARGARET CHASE SMITH

Although occupational burnout can happen in any profession, caregiving careers run a higher risk of developing compassion fatigue. The combined effects of being on-call around the clock, delicately handling death, and working with the bereaved can easily take their toll. Have you ever felt burned out?

*

STEPHEN BARON
Stephen is a 64-year-old funeral service
licensee in Grand Haven, Michigan

I think I have experienced the earlier stages of burnout, but have never felt the total lack of interest, energy and imagination that I understand comes with it. While I recognize the fact that true burnout happens to some in any profession, what I experienced more than once in my career were times when there was a lack of focus. Times when it was crucial for me to reassess what I was doing and re-prioritize commitments in how I was addressing them. Over the years, I have found a need to slow it down, take some self-inventory of what I am doing and if needed, ask others to help.

What it really comes down to is the need to do an "emotion check." When you constantly deal with people at one of the hardest times in their lives, you have moments when you start to question your own ability to feel. When those times present themselves, it is a good idea to back down a bit and realize that you are human too, and perhaps you have reached your limit for a time. This awareness of myself has helped me stay in the game and be both more proficient and efficient in my work.

*

CHASTIN BRINKLEY
Chastin is a 47-year-old funeral director, embalmer
and cremation specialist in Buckley, Washington

I have never felt burned out so to speak. The first funeral home where I worked, I was paid four dollars an hour and after three days I was making time and a half. At that time, I only had one suit. After about three weeks of employment, I asked the owner if I could have a day off so I could get my suit dry cleaned. He said, "No, just wear jeans tomorrow."

In the nine months I worked there, I don't think I had more than ten days off. I probably would have joined a union back then just so I could get a day off.

If I was to offer advice to fellow funeral directors to prevent burnout, it would be to make sure to get time away from work. Seek a funeral home with a good schedule with guaranteed time off. Usually, larger funeral homes have better schedules. I know of a funeral home where there are only two funeral directors. They rotate being on night call, two nights in a row. That is a tough on-call schedule, even for very dedicated funeral directors. However, such is the nature of the business.

*

JENNI BRYANT
Jenni is a 41-year-old funeral director
and embalmer in Maryville, Tennessee

I have been a licensed funeral director and embalmer for a little over sixteen years. I have worked at the same funeral home for my whole career. I personally have never experienced burnout. I do, however, work with a few people who I believe have, or are currently experiencing, burnout. I believe the reason that I have not felt burnout is because I do my best to take care of myself mentally. I surround myself with good people and take time to re-energize myself. My bosses also realize that there is a high rate of burnout in the funeral industry and they have taken several precautions to help us prevent burnout. They have created a work schedule that gives us plenty of time off, they encourage us to take our breaks and lunches away from the funeral home, and they give us paid vacation time every year, and encourage us to use it. I personally am very involved with several funeral industry groups that promote continuing education. I feel that this is one of the things that I do to prevent burnout myself. I enjoy going to these meetings and talking with other funeral directors, getting ideas, and discussing things that are sometimes hard for people who are not in the funeral business to understand.

*

LAUREN BUDROW
Lauren is a 44-year-old funeral director
and funeral service educator

At the end of my internship year I was depressed. I was crying at inappropriate times, having dreams of deceased people I had buried, and was struggling emotionally. It took me several months to figure out how to compartmentalize my feelings and to stop feeling as if I was carrying a sack of grief on me like a backpack. Working at a high-volume location doesn't make things easier when you're new to the profession, quite the opposite. The lack of downtime resulted in my feeling overwhelmed by constant death and emotional overload from families who counted on me to be their rock. I swung the other way and started to feel numb and uncaring as I was trying to figure out how to balance my feelings with the realities of my career.

However, my coworkers and I always felt that if we stopped feeling anything for our families, then we had overstayed our time in the business. That line of burnout rests somewhere between caring too much and feeling nothing. Part of my internship struggle was that I was given no vacation time, and I felt depressed and empty in a very short period of time. Breaks are essential to sustaining a caring attitude toward families and maintaining a healthy balance personally.

*

JASON RYAN ENGLER
Jason is a 36-year-old funeral director, certified celebrant,
and cremation historian in Rogers, Arkansas

I have faced burnout on several occasions. The intensity of the emotion we come in contact with can often be draining and if we fail to take time to rest and regain our focus, it can be detrimental to our well-being, and our ability to serve others. I often come into contact with funeral professionals who are facing burnout. We all know that this profession can easily weigh on our minds and bodies so that it makes it difficult to offer empathy and sympathy. I am firmly convinced though, that there is too much to gain to give up on the care we give those in most need of our support.

*

SHARON GEE-MASCARELLO
Sharon is a 53-year-old funeral director and embalming instructor
in the Mortuary Science Program at Wayne State University in Detroit

Career burnout is real. I faced burnout immediately after the death of my mom. When I returned to work, I struggled to give one hundred percent of my focus to the family sitting across from me. I stood up, walked around my desk and pulled up a chair next to them. We finished the arrangement and I stopped meeting with families that day. I realized that my own grief was a liability. I was certain that I could no longer afford to give away one hundred percent and my families didn't deserve less than my full attention. A full year later, I returned to the arrangement office. My advice: listen to yourself. You know best.

*

LOUISE GOHMANN
Louise is a 61-year-old mortuary school educator
and funeral director in Jeffersonville, Indiana

I have never really felt burned out, but have felt exceedingly empty, tired physically and spiritually. It always seems that when I've reached a low point, a family comes along who fills me right back up.

*

KAREN JELLY
Karen is a 44-year-old funeral director
and mortician in Havre, Montana

I consistently feel burned out. I work for a small town, family-owned funeral home. The funeral service industry is either feast or famine, with me on-call year-round. During the feast times, I get very little rest, as I am removing people and embalming through the night on a regular basis. I then meet with the families the next day and plan the services. Then I perform all the duties involved in executing a truly personalized service for the family. During the famine times, I catch up on paperwork (which I am trying to do at all times), and perform all the maintenance and upkeep tasks I don't have time for during the feast times.

At all times, however, the emotional rewards I receive helping families is what keeps me going, no matter how stressed or burned out I feel. I am also fortunate in that, when I feel burned out, I can talk with my manager, who is also my friend. We vent to each other to help reduce stress. In addition, she tries to find ways to help me get away from work a few days here and there, so that I can recharge. If you are facing burnout, find a hobby you can really get into, whether it be golf, flying model airplanes, crocheting or knitting, or gardening. That recharge time is vital to your mental health.

*

CODY JONES
Cody is a 37-year-old progressive funeral home owner
and funeral director in Bryan-College Station, Texas

Burnout is mentioned frequently in the funeral profession, mostly because we work in a twenty-four-hour business, and because there are many funeral directors who are dedicated to the families they serve. Thankfully, I enjoy my job and our profession, so I haven't reached the burnout point—at least not yet—this early in my short funeral career of thirteen years. As an owner, I emphasize to my staff that I do not want them to reach that point either. I believe everyone deserves time off to be with their families, to go on vacation, or just to have some time to be away from the stresses that come with serving families day in and day out.

*

CORIANN MARTIN
Coriann is a 42-year-old funeral director
and embalmer in Kenosha, Wisconsin

I think we all agree we can get burned out more than once in our career. I hit my first rough patch when I was rounding out my apprenticeship, and really struggled with my career choice. After making a decision to move to a new city, however, I found a renewed energy about funeral service. I had a great support system of coworkers and a boss who let me be as creative as I wanted. I really gained an immense amount of experience and a sense of rejuvenation being somewhere new and with people who shared my passion.

I hit another rough patch five years later when I was married and had compromised with my husband-to-be about where we should live. I made the move again to a small town and really had difficulties adjusting. My job took the brunt of my frustration and I actually left funeral service for about six months. While I was away from what I loved doing, I had an epiphany that it was time to return. I decided to never allow anyone or any circumstance to dictate my future.

I think we all need to take inventory of what we are doing. We have a very stressful job and the pressure can build up. It makes us question what we're doing and can sometimes make us want to give up. There is no way to avoid the stress of a career that has such high standards. I just find that we need to keep a positive perspective of what's important in life because if there is anyone who knows how quickly life can be taken away from you, it's us.

*

LACY ROBINSON
Lacy is a 38-year-old Director of Member Development for the
National Funeral Directors Association in Brookfield, Wisconsin

I've met many funeral directors over the years who have experienced burnout. When this happens, it not only impacts one's job performance but one's personal relationships and health as well. Highly driven funeral directors may find themselves overcommitting to community events or professional organizations all while serving families twenty-four hours a day for weeks at a time with no time off. I encourage funeral home owners and managers to build their dream team of employees they can count on to give one hundred percent every single day. When the right team is in place, responsibilities can be delegated with confidence. It's about leveraging the strengths of every employee. This will prevent job burnout as well as maintain strong motivation to exceed the expectations of every family served.

*

SHAWNA RODABAUGH
Shawna is a 37-year-old funeral director and
embalmer in Mount Pleasant, Michigan

I think that at some point, all directors reach a point when they feel burned out. There are long hours involved and high emotions. For me, when I got to the point when I felt I couldn't handle it anymore, I took time to remember why I'm working. Sometimes I would actually go into the preparation room and spend time with some of the loved ones, remembering the stories their families had told me, and just take the moment to appreciate their life.

*

STEVE TWEEDLE
Steve is a 42-year-old funeral
director in Ocala, Florida

I've been working at a funeral home in some capacity for twenty-five years. I have never felt burned out. I hope that I will get out of the business if I ever do. Don't get me wrong, there are days when I don't want to go to work, days when I'm tired, or stressed out. But I've never had the experience of being on autopilot, or just going through the motions. I recently learned that I sometimes need to take a break. If I feel myself getting tired and nothing is going on, I'll leave the office to run to the local store and buy a big bag of chocolate and start handing it out around the office. I also created a stress bag for the office. If I see my staff getting stressed, we break out the stress bag. I have a ten and a twelve-year-old. I give them a dollar amount and let them loose in a dollar store. They come back with candy, coloring books, bubbles, all kinds of silly little knickknacks for the stress bag. When things get hectic, the staff has to close their eyes and reach in; what they grab, they keep. It's fun to watch what they get and how they react, and I've found that bubble blowing is very therapeutic.

*

BRIAN VAN HECK
Brian is a 41-year-old funeral director in
the Lake Norman area of North Carolina

Being a man of faith, I choose to view my profession not simply as just a job but truly a ministry to people in a time of great need. As with caregiving and ministry professions, many funeral directors do experience burnout. We also see an incredibly high rate of alcoholism. I have been blessed in my career to work for funeral homes that were always adequately staffed and allowed me to work a scheduled number of days, evenings, weekends and an on-call rotation, but most importantly, days off. Given the intense nature and highly emotional work we do, time away is crucial to our well-being.

I learned the importance of disengaging early on in my career at the first funeral home I worked in as a funeral director assistant during graduate school. This particular firm had multiple locations and served over 1,200 families annually, meaning there was always a great deal happening. Every morning after a couple hours of work, those staff members that were able, would take about a thirty minute coffee break to chat about life and miscellaneous topics, but most importantly to disengage from our work with the dead and the bereaved. As I continued in my career, I realized the importance of disengaging from what we, as funeral directors and funeral home employees, do on a daily basis. It is critical for our overall emotional health to connect with the living even if it is in a superficial way.

There have been times, even in a well-staffed funeral home, when the number and intensity of families has taken its toll on me and I have not always taken the best care of myself. I fell victim to alcohol during my career but am grateful to have overcame that nine years ago. Through my recovery, I've been able to recognize and integrate emotional, physical and spiritual strategies to reduce burnout. Emotionally, I have men outside my profession who I connect with regularly. Physically, I eat a healthy diet, strength train and participate in competitive slalom skiing. Spiritually, I have an active prayer life, read scripture and attend church regularly. Additionally, I am very aware of what I put into my brain via television, radio, social media and internet. These habits have helped me become the best version of myself that I can, and as a result, the best funeral director I can be.

*

KIMBERLY VARELA
Kimberly is a 41-year-old funeral director
and embalmer in Westland, Michigan

I've felt burned out mostly on an emotional level. Some days we feel we can't give anymore, or what we're giving isn't good enough. Dealing with tragedy, sadness, grief and trauma are mentally and emotionally taxing. What really takes the wind out of our sails is family members who use us as an emotional crutch. Either they don't want to deal with grief on their own, or they use our position as a sounding board, grief counselor, gossip partner and personal errand runner. I've had families unabashedly tell me the most intimate details of their lives. Calls at 3 a.m. to inquire about minor details are not uncommon. I love my families but some require more handholding.

*

DAN WELCH
Dan is a 30-year-old funeral director and
embalmer in Wichita, Kansas

Having been in the business full-time for roughly six years, I cannot say that I have ever felt burned out. However, I occasionally, like most jobs, find myself longing for that day off or that vacation. I feel one of the main reasons I have been blessed to avoid burnout is because I make a point to create "me" time on a regular basis. I know that this can be difficult at times, but at the end of the day, I have found that if I am unable to take care of myself, there is no way I will be able to adequately take care of the families who call upon my services.

CHAPTER EIGHT

Memorable Moments

Obviously, the most memorable has a lot to do with
the time spent on the matter. -CATHERINE CRIER

Weird stuff happens in every career, but can become commonplace in the funeral industry. High emotions can lead to family fistfights, mix ups can lead to the wrong viewing, and broken equipment at the worst time can lead to unforgettable moments. What's the funniest situation or most memorable experienced you've had in your career?

*

STEPHEN BARON
Stephen is a 64-year-old funeral service
licensee in Grand Haven, Michigan

The most memorable experience of my career and also without question, the highest honor, was when our firm was called upon to help coordinate and plan local funeral and entombment services for the thirty-eighth president of the United States, Gerald R. Ford. Over the past several generations, the Ford family has called upon our firm many times to serve their family and extended family. What many people are not aware of is the fact that the planning and organization that goes into state funerals, usually begins years in advance of the death. In this case, planning began when the president left office in 1977, and continued until the time of his death in 2006. Meetings were held two or three times a year. Included in these meetings were, of course, government officials and all the organizations that were to be directly involved in the execution of the ceremony. Logistics varied according to the scenario presented, down to the place of death, to if the president's spouse had or had not predeceased him. To fully describe this experience in total would take pages. Suffice it to say, my involvement in the process was truly an honor, especially knowing that this honor has been shared with only a few of my profession over the past 240 years.

As in any type of work, there will always be days when nothing seems to go right. Among those days, hopefully some of those happenings will be laced with treasured and memorable humor. Funeral service, simply by the serious nature of most situations, is not immune to a humorous side. It has been my experience however, that in most of these cases, it is only your staff who gets to see the full humor of these faux pas. Mourners are usually oblivious because of their emotions and diverted attentions. Many of these experiences that I have been witness to, probably would not seem all that funny to a grieving person. That being said, I will resist answering with specifics.

*

CHASTIN BRINKLEY
Chastin is a 47-year-old funeral director, embalmer
and cremation specialist in Buckley, Washington

There are funny stories shared at funerals, but to me death is not funny. I do have a recurring nightmare in which I'm driving the funeral coach to the cemetery. The sun is setting, it's getting dark and I can't find the cemetery. No matter where I turn, I still can't find it. I know how the owner feels about employees being late for a service, and I fear losing my job. When I wake up, my heart is pounding, the sheets are soaked with sweat, and I feel exhausted. Later, I joke with our office coordinator who is responsible for payroll that the funeral home owes me a few hours of pay for dreaming about work.

*

LAUREN BUDROW
Lauren is a 44-year-old funeral director
and funeral service educator

I was still in my internship when I answered the phone at the funeral home. It was 4:30 p.m. and I had already met two families and set up a visitation that day. I was tired and eager to go home. After I picked up the phone and went through the usual greeting I heard, "Do you have things at your place that I can touch and feel?"

I was caught off guard and asked the woman to repeat herself, which she did. When I explained to her that we had casket samples she could indeed touch and feel, she said, "We're down the street and we're on our way." It seemed I was not going home anytime soon.

This woman, her two children and daughter-in-law walked in to the funeral home after driving down from a competitor up the street. For the next two and a half hours we planned her husband's funeral. At the conclusion of it, we were all quite tired and a bit punchy. The lady said to me, "When I called, I didn't think you knew what you were doing."

To that I responded, "When I answered the phone, I thought you were crazy."

We stayed friends for many years after that and I attended her daughter's wedding. At the reception, this woman introduced me as her funeral director. It was silly and yet the best feeling in the world.

*

SHARON GEE-MASCARELLO
Sharon is a 53-year-old funeral director and embalming instructor
in the Mortuary Science Program at Wayne State University in Detroit

A very close call...

Following a busy morning of dressing and casketing, the decedent was placed in state for first visitation. I scanned one last time from the back of the chapel to be certain that everything was as it should be. Then, I felt a rush of air as my colleague raced past me and down the steps to the prep room. In an instant he reappeared and pointed to his wrist, a strange look on his face. "Where is my watch?" he shouted. Our eyes met and without a word we both sprinted to the casket. He retrieved his watch simultaneous to the chime of the doorbell as the family entered for first visitation.

*

LOUISE GOHMANN
Louise is a 61-year-old mortuary school educator
and funeral director in Jeffersonville, Indiana

An old gentleman from the Kentucky mountain country died, and it fell to my friend, and fellow funeral director, and I to take him to his final resting place, his family cemetery in a small town in eastern Kentucky. The family told us it was rough country, and suggested that jeans and boots would be appropriate attire. Our coworkers teased us and reminded us to watch for bears. We drove the four hours to meet the family, and arrived at a little white church with a lovely little cemetery in the church yard. "This isn't so bad," we thought, and stepped out to do the burial.

"Where's the grave?" I asked, looking around.

"Oh, it's not here," a son said. "It's up there," and he pointed into the woods and up to the mountains. I must have looked distressed, because a grandson said, "Don't worry Miss Lee. My dad brought his gun."

"Is that for the bears?" asked my friend.

"No," replied the grandson cheerfully. "It's for the rattlesnakes!"

It took nine of us switching off to get the casket to the top of the mountain. At one point the casket was vertical as we huffed and puffed and made our way up. The gentleman's wife, a spry octogenarian, led the way. She nearly ran up to the top! When we finally got there, the casket was lowered with ropes into his family ground. I swore I could hear him sigh with pleasure as we laid him next to his parents. As we stood there after the minister finished the prayer, his wife said, "Well, I guess the next time y'all come up here it will be to carry me."

Her son put a companionable arm around her and said, "Mama, have you ever considered cremation?"

*

KAREN JELLY
Karen is a 44-year-old funeral director
and mortician in Havre, Montana

I've had many memorable experiences in my career, although I don't know that any of them would be considered funny. Families grieve in different ways, and grief affects each individual differently. Many of the experiences that I've had cannot be recounted in this book due to confidentiality.

However, in the funeral home where I was the office manager, I distinctly remember a family where the sisters were arguing over the disposition of their unmarried brother, and two of them headed out to the front lawn where they proceeded to have a little bout of fisticuffs before the final decision was made. As soon as they started throwing punches, the girls were told in no uncertain terms that continuation on this course would result in law enforcement intervention. It ended as soon as it began. That situation will forever rest in my mind.

I also had the honor of caring for a fifteen-year-old young man. His mother and father were wonderful, and I was able to help make his funeral all it could be. That service is the reason I cannot listen to "The Dance," by Garth Brooks without crying.

I have to say that all the services I handle are memorable for the families, and that is what is important to me... that the families believe we've provided them with a service that is tailored to their loved one.

*

CODY JONES
Cody is a 37-year-old progressive funeral home owner
and funeral director in Bryan-College Station, Texas

A funny moment that comes to mind involves my dad and grandfather. Most people know that funeral directors sometimes have to cut the back of the clothing when dressing the body. One day, my dad could not find his suit jacket and looked everywhere for it. As it turns out, he had hung it in the back room and forgot about it. My grandfather mistakenly cut it and used it to dress the body. No wonder my dad couldn't find his suit coat! Thankfully they realized it before the visitation.

*

CORIANN MARTIN
Coriann is a 42-year-old funeral director
and embalmer in Kenosha, Wisconsin

It seems so weird to talk about a funny funeral when it is such a sensitive topic but we've all had those moments. I remember the funeral for the cousin of a good friend of mine. Although he died way too young, he was apparently quite the character. His funeral was the typical traditional funeral: visitation at night, funeral the next day at his parish, followed by the burial in a local cemetery. But, what we all weren't expecting when we exited the chapel at the cemetery was for the song "It Takes Two" by Rob Base and DJ E-Z Rock to be blaring from the bell tower speakers. The family explained that anytime he was at a family wedding or get-together, he just had to get on the dance floor when that song played. It was a very fitting tribute to him and made everyone leave with a smile on their face.

*

LACY ROBINSON
Lacy is a 38-year-old Director of Member Development for the
National Funeral Directors Association in Brookfield, Wisconsin

When I was just starting out in funeral service, I was driving the brand new Cadillac limousine on a country road. The grieving family sat in the back and another family member sat next to me. We had just left the committal service, and a huge truck came toward us hauling a double wide trailer. In my mind, this truck was coming at us head-on. I was a ball of nerves, and was sweating and shaking. I decided in that moment, the best thing for me to do was pull off the road. Just as I started to pull off, I knew it was a mistake because everyone in the limousine slid to the right. I was now looking down at the family member beside me. The grieving family had to get out and push the limousine and me back up onto the road as their friends and family were driving past us.

I also remember getting pulled over at 2 a.m. while driving the funeral home's van. I admit I was going a little fast. I had just left from meeting one family at a hospital and was heading to meet a second family at a nursing home. My adrenaline was on high. What made this incident even more interesting was that I was pulled over just as I was making my way into the funeral home parking lot. Instead of waiting for the police officer to come to my vehicle, I jumped out and ordered him to turn off his lights. I then proceeded to ask him if he was aware of how busy the funeral home had been lately. I was sure he had not been reading the obituaries. I was a woman on a mission that night and nothing was going to stop me. Fortunately, I did not receive a ticket and I felt as though the police officer appreciated my sense of urgency in serving the community.

*

SHAWNA RODABAUGH
Shawna is a 37-year-old funeral director and
embalmer in Mount Pleasant, Michigan

Although nothing overly funny comes to mind, I have had plenty of memorable services throughout my career. One that stays with me is the service of a young man who lost his life while he was putting gas in his car at the side of a highway. He had small children and a wife, and it was a great challenge to make him presentable so that his family could see him to say goodbye. When the family walked into the chapel to view him, I had never seen such pain and gratitude, all at the same time. That is everything I work for.

*

STEVE TWEEDLE
Steve is a 42-year-old funeral
director in Ocala, Florida

I remember funny situations that happen behind the scenes more than anything. My boss wore a toupee. He wasn't a vain person; he wore it to prevent skin cancer. We were at a large funeral in a local church. There were people everywhere. The boss always came to visit with people but had a certain set of standards. He would stop you in the middle of what you were doing to make sure those standards were met. His other standard was that his hair was combed and not a mess. He was an old and proper Southern gentleman who believed you should always look your best when going out.

At the funeral, people were walking around when he appeared out of nowhere, as he often did, and asked me (at least I thought), "How many people are here?"

I said, "I don't know, 350 to 400 people."

He paused, looked at me and said, "What did I ask you?"

I replied, "You asked me how many people are here."

He said, "No. I asked you, how's my hair?"

It's one of those moments when you just stop and laugh. You have all of this going on; at that moment the weight of the world is on your shoulders, and I got asked how his hair was.

We hired one of my best friends to work for us. We had known each other since kindergarten. My friend is a conspiracy theorist to say the least. He's super intelligent but believes the government is listening to everything we say and do, aliens have infiltrated us and are among us observing, and Bigfoot is real. One early evening, he was bringing a decedent under our care and had backed the removal vehicle up to the garage stall. He brought the decedent out of the vehicle and was completing the paperwork when all of a sudden he heard the door slam on the removal vehicle and it peeled out of the parking area.

Now keep in mind that we had funeral directors living on the property and were pulling a prank. They had hidden and waited for him to come back. As soon as he got to where he couldn't see the vehicle and they knew the decedent was out, they jumped in and took off. They pulled around the corner, parked the car, and returned on bikes they had hidden.

In the time it took for them to do that, my friend had called the police, the owner of the funeral home, and his immediate supervisor. He was standing all disheveled in the parking lot holding a huge lead pipe like a baseball bat, waiting for the villains to come back. As the two funeral directors rode up on their bikes, they found the local police department pulling in with them. After a few minutes of confusion and a lots of explaining, they finally convinced everyone they were the culprits. The cops eventually found it funny, but warned us not to do it again.

*

BRIAN VAN HECK
Brian is a 41-year-old funeral director in
the Lake Norman area of North Carolina

After I decided to answer my life's call and dedicate my life to funeral service, I was hired back full-time by the funeral home where I had worked while in graduate school. They created a position for me as an arrangement counselor which meant I would be doing everything a funeral director did except for physical preparation of the body (embalming). Namely, it meant I would be meeting with families to make funeral arrangements but there were certain aspects of a licensed funeral director's position that I could not perform due to state law.

While I had been working in and around funeral homes for a few years at that point, sitting face to face with families in the arrangement conference room was an experience I didn't yet have. After spending a couple weeks shadowing seasoned funeral directors conducting the arrangement process, I was cut loose to meet with my first family. The mid-morning appointment time had been set by the funeral director who was on-call the night before. I would be meeting with an elderly gentleman whose wife had died. I had a relatively high level of anxiety masked beneath my presentation of confidence and professionalism. I navigated my way through the paperwork and conversation about planning the funeral mass for his wife.

Next, it was time to take him into the casket selection room for him to choose the casket. After a few moments in the room, he indicated that he would like the solid copper casket. I was somewhat in disbelief but knew I could not express that emotional response. The copper casket was the second most expensive casket in that room and this was my first arrangement ever. I knew the veteran funeral directors were going to have some commentary for this. I did not enter this profession to sell caskets, however not a bad way to start. Any bit of confidence that might have been heightened by this gentleman's selection quickly vanished when we made our way back to the conference room. I was reviewing the financial contract with him and could not even remember his name! That was an incredibly embarrassing and awkward moment. And so began my work as a funeral arranger.

While that experience was more embarrassing than funny, there have been a plethora of funny, memorable and unique moments throughout my tenure as a funeral director thus far. There was the woman who requested we place her husband's cremated remains in a two liter Mountain Dew bottle because that was his favorite drink. However, when they didn't all fit, she had to go to the corner gas station and obtain a twenty-ounce bottle to accommodate the rest of his remains. There were the dates that I've gone on with granddaughters after working their grandmother's funerals, at their request not mine. My wife is not one of the grieving granddaughters (in case you were wondering). Trying to maintain professional composure as a family legitimately and seriously inquired about getting their loved one's pacemaker back because "it was only three weeks old and they might be able to sell it."

*

KIMBERLY VARELA
Kimberly is a 41-year-old funeral director
and embalmer in Westland, Michigan

As I was escorting a family from our upstairs arrangement office, I heard someone ask me a question. I turned to answer and didn't realize I was so close to the first step on the stairs. Before I knew it I was brass over teakettle down seven stairs to the first landing. Everyone of course collectively gasped and I immediately jumped up as if I had stuck the landing at the 2016 Olympics, shouting, "I'm alright!" Ironically we had just been talking about how one of the family members had a recent knee replacement and wanted to go down the stairs last to take her time. We had joked that if she fell, she would have plenty of people to cushion her at the bottom. I led the family out and waved as they pulled away. Only then did I limp back to my office to ice my bumps and bruises, and my pride.

*

DAN WELCH
Dan is a 30-year-old funeral director and
embalmer in Wichita, Kansas

By far the funniest experience I have ever had at a funeral took place in early 2016. We were at a small Catholic church in a small farm town. As we were preparing to process in for mass, the wheelchair-bound grandfather of the deceased began to proclaim his need to use the restroom. Unfortunately, the church did not have a handicap accessible bathroom. For nearly ten minutes, myself, two other directors and a pallbearer attempted to assist this elderly man into the restroom with no success. Eventually, the priest came to us and told us we needed to start the service, and that the elderly man in the wheelchair would just have to hold it.

About halfway through mass, I noticed the elderly man hunched over in the chair for about thirty seconds before he sat up. Within moments, we all suddenly realized that urine was flowing from all sides of the wheelchair and pooling into the aisle around the casket. As the mass continued, the priest and the altar servers repeatedly walked through the urine. Each time they took a step, their shoes squeaked on the marble floor, echoing throughout the church. By the end of mass, everyone knew what had happened, and the priest felt quite sheepish.

*

There may be no single thing that can
teach us more about life than death.

ARIANNA HUFFINGTON

*

CHAPTER NINE

Societal Reactions

I have found that I get a better reaction from people once I am less bothered about their reaction. -WILLIAM HAGUE

When asked, most people readily share what they do for a living. But admitting one works in the funeral industry opens the door for myriad of reactions ranging from shock to curiosity. What's the most memorable reaction you've received when you told someone you were a funeral director?

*

STEPHEN BARON
Stephen is a 64-year-old funeral service
licensee in Grand Haven, Michigan

When I was young and was asked what my father did for a living, my stock answer was that he owned a body shop, and most always that was the end of the discussion. After all, how interesting is taking dents out of fenders? Later, after I was licensed, I realized that this question never stopped and I thought I was smart by answering that I was in

"Underground Novelties." That answer seldom worked and I found myself fessing up that I was a funeral director, embalmer, or both.

The truthful answer has been met with every kind of reaction you can think of. Usually a disgusted snort or a change of subject. A colleague of mine was seated on an airplane waiting to leave the gate when the lady next to him asked the question. When he gave the truthful answer, the lady simply turned and asked the flight attendant to change her seat.

My favorite response to my answer came from a middle-aged woman who responded with, "Oh, so you truly are an angel sent from above." I was both surprised and very pleased.

*

CHASTIN BRINKLEY
Chastin is a 47-year-old funeral director, embalmer
and cremation specialist in Buckley, Washington

The most common reaction I receive when I tell someone that I am a funeral director and embalmer is, "Oh." Then the person will start sharing with me his or her experience they had at a funeral home. Most of the experiences shared are positive. Every now and then, when I tell someone what I do for a living, they say, "Well, I guess someone has to do it." That statement bothers me because I don't have to be a funeral director. No one forced me into this profession. I chose to be a funeral director.

*

JENNI BRYANT
Jenni is a 41-year-old funeral director
and embalmer in Maryville, Tennessee

Being a woman and a funeral director and embalmer usually gets a strange reaction from people. The majority of people say, "There is no way I could do what you do!" or " I'm glad there are people like you around," or something corny like, "So, you'll be the last one to let me down!" And then there are those who have a million questions. They want to know all the details and everything involved in an embalming. I love it when I am driving the hearse and people look over, then do a double take when they realize a woman is driving.

*

LAUREN BUDROW
Lauren is a 44-year-old funeral director
and funeral service educator

The responses to telling someone I'm in funeral service are:

1. "Someone has to do it." Well yes, I suppose that's true. It's such a demeaning statement though. I feel that way about wastewater treatment or animal insemination but I don't say it to those people who do those jobs.

2. "It takes a special person." Meaning what exactly? Aren't all people special in one way or another? The definition of special seems to take on something that feels less than other professions when used in this context.

3. "I guess it's job security." Well, only if every single person who dies comes to your firm for your entire career.

4. "So folks are dying to see you?" Ha, ha. Yeah, never heard that one before.

I suppose it's how people respond when faced with an awkward topic. If you're wondering, yes, we have heard all the jokes.

*

JASON RYAN ENGLER
Jason is a 36-year-old funeral director, certified celebrant,
and cremation historian in Rogers, Arkansas

From years of experience, I have found that personal wishes are one of the most common discussions I have when friends and family discover that I am a funeral and cremation professional. Recently, during a conversation with a friend (who happens to be younger than me), the inevitable conversation came up. "I don't want anyone to be sad when I die. Just take my ashes and scatter them to the wind and throw a huge party." I sat looking at him in honest surprise. I couldn't even begin to fathom the depth of the conversation that could have occurred in that moment, but the sheer overwhelming moment of argument passed gently through me. After all, everyone is entitled to their own ideas, their own wishes. I've heard the comment, but unfortunately it is more and more common.

Wouldn't it be nice to never be sad when someone dies, plodding along through life unfazed by the loss of a friend or relative or coworker or other member of society? Make it a tidy affair with no muss and no fuss. Make the body disappear and the grief along with it. Right? It really isn't that easy.

While death is often met with grace and dignity by the dying, it is usually met with grief and sadness by the survivors. This is still so after thousands upon thousands of years of people dying, and recognizing that death brings sadness. It isn't an emotion that we choose... it just is. The strange truth, however, is that sadness is normal. This unwanted, undesired, unappreciated, emotion is a natural part of the human psyche and an important part of the grieving process.

*

SHARON GEE-MASCARELLO
Sharon is a 53-year-old funeral director and embalming instructor
in the Mortuary Science Program at Wayne State University in Detroit

When asked, I tell folks that I'm a final events planner. Usually, this takes a few moments to sink in. Most laugh. Then comes the epiphany: "Ahhhh, I never thought of death that way, but I guess that the funeral really is life's final event." And then the typical addendum: "I guess someone has to do it." To which I respond, "I didn't choose to become a funeral director, the vocation chose me." I then insert my personal story about how I was led to help others for a living. I believe I dispel mystery, create value, and make a friend this way. And, I never overlook an opportunity to provide education.

Given the whole story, people will come to their own conclusions about what we do. This is just a gentle nudge to help them see it from our perspective. Kimberly Varela's poem, "I Hold Things," tells our story best. I've made it my quest to put her poem in every funeral home lobby for colleagues and families alike.

*

LOUISE GOHMANN
Louise is a 61-year-old mortuary school educator
and funeral director in Jeffersonville, Indiana

When I told my friends and family that I was going to be a funeral director, the reaction was mostly hoots of laughter or disbelief. When I've met someone new, I've had people take a step back, or shudder. The usual response is, "I could never do that!" I asked my students to share about the first time they got "the look." One student said she was shaking hands with someone, and he literally pulled his hand away and wiped it on his trousers, as if he would catch something!

*

KAREN JELLY
Karen is a 44-year-old funeral director
and mortician in Havre, Montana

The most memorable reaction I've had when I was asked what I do is the funniest look of shock, as though someone who is personable, upbeat, and funny cannot be a mortician. It really cracks me up! The most common reaction I receive is usually people pulling away a little, as though the sadness I am surrounded with every day will rub off. That is, until they get to know me better. Then they realize that I'm just a person who is involved in what is an often very demanding career.

I am bothered by some reactions I get. One of those reactions is what I call the "you're a horrible person" reaction. Those who react this way will often say things like, "How can you do that to people?" or "Why do you want to hurt families like that?" I believe these people truly do not understand what I do or how I do it. Or, they have been hurt by an unethical, unscrupulous, or just bad funeral director in the past, and don't understand that there are people like me out there to help, not hurt.

*

CODY JONES
Cody is a 37-year-old progressive funeral home owner
and funeral director in Bryan-College Station, Texas

When I first met my wife, Chelsea, I told her I was a funeral director when she asked what I did. She didn't believe me and she just thought I was playing a joke. Joke was on her though, because in just a few months she was helping with hair and makeup!

*

CORIANN MARTIN
Coriann is a 42-year-old funeral director
and embalmer in Kenosha, Wisconsin

I have to say that every time I tell someone what I do for a living, I almost always get the same reaction. They walk up to me, a young woman, about five feet tall who looks to be in her twenties (okay, maybe thirties) and they ask me what I do for a living. Hearing that I'm a funeral director and embalmer makes them take a step back and say, "Oh, wow. How did you get into that?" Honestly, sometimes I don't want to answer the slew of questions that follow, so I lie. It's not out of embarrassment, but I can usually tell if people are truly interested in what I do or if they are just looking for the gory details.

*

LACY ROBINSON
Lacy is a 38-year-old Director of Member Development for the National Funeral Directors Association in Brookfield, Wisconsin

Usually when I mention I'm in funeral service, I receive a surprised look from people. Next to follow is the question, "How did you get into that?" It's always an interesting conversation and typically ends with the person sharing with me their funeral home experiences.

*

SHAWNA RODABAUGH
Shawna is a 37-year-old funeral director and
embalmer in Mount Pleasant, Michigan

When I was younger, I was at the bar with a few friends, and we were meeting new people. The typical question always comes up: "What do you do?" This time when I answered that I was a funeral director, the gentleman I was talking to immediately stopped talking, put his drink down, and walked right out of the bar. The running joke with my friends after that was that if I ever wanted someone to leave me alone, I just had to mention my work.

I get a span of reactions when I tell people what I do, and most of them are kind and appreciative, but the ones that bother me are the invasive questions about the body, and what happens after death. It doesn't bother me that the questions come up, but the amount of misinformation about what we do, and what happens to the human body after death, is astounding. I correct what I can when I hear it, but misinformation is still everywhere.

*

STEVE TWEEDLE
Steve is a 42-year-old funeral
director in Ocala, Florida

Most people react the same way. They take a step back. My favorite, and I think, the funniest response, is when they ask in a low tone, "Do you see dead people?" They always look around like they are passing on some secret of national security as they ask. I ask them if they've ever been to McDonald's and seen a hamburger. It's funny because nine times out of ten you get that, "Aha!" moment when they realize what they just asked. I've had some people turn and walk away. I've had some people refuse to shake my hand. None of those reactions bother me. I get it. What I do makes people uncomfortable. It makes them face their greatest fear, and their mortality. The reactions that bother me the most are when people tell me a negative experience they've had at a funeral home. I don't like hearing about someone who is in this profession misrepresenting what we do.

*

BRIAN VAN HECK
Brian is a 41-year-old funeral director in
the Lake Norman area of North Carolina

For as much of a death denying culture as we live in, there is a unique fascination and intrigue with death. One need only experience the rubbernecking and traffic backup when there is a serious crash on our highways and byways. Similarly, when we are at a party, on an airplane or in any situation with individuals we do not know, within ten to fifteen minutes of conversation the question, "So, what do you do?" undoubtedly arises. The litany of questions that follow when the answer is, "I am a funeral director," varies but the conversation never ends there.

I have chosen to use these times as a way to educate the individual on my profession, candidly and honestly answering their questions. Most people have not met or had professional dealings with a funeral director, so I want to represent my profession in the best possible way. Most importantly, I want to give them accurate and honest information because there is so much misinformation and myths in and around what we do. Common responses include: "I don't know how you do what you do," "I couldn't do that," and "Isn't it depressing?" In these moments, I allow myself to share my story, beliefs and thoughts, and accurately answer any question they might have.

*

KIMBERLY VARELA
Kimberly is a 41-year-old funeral director
and embalmer in Westland, Michigan

I was approached in a grocery store and asked why I was dressed so nicely in my black skirt suit at 12 a.m. in the morning. I had just worked a fourteen-hour shift that included a service, visitation, arrangement and embalming all in one day and I was exhausted. I looked the man straight in the face and told him I was a funeral director thinking it would shut down the conversation immediately. Most people are on one side of the spectrum or another. I've found no middle ground. You get the "Ew, gross!" crowd or the "Oooh, that's so interesting, tell me more," crowd. Unfortunately I had encountered the latter.

Instead of shutting him down, it turned into a strange approach at hitting on me. He told me a story about how he loved crime shows (a. I'm not a pathologist; b. Don't try to pick me up in a grocery store at midnight with the line of "I watch a lot of crime shows about murder and it gets me to thinking"). He also told me he liked *The Walking Dead*, which I do too, but proceeded to tell me he would know just what to do if a zombie apocalypse ever happened. He thought it would be a good idea for us to be a team since I know about death and decomposition rates and where to avoid crowds of zombies. I finally had to pull out the old, "I should call my husband because it's getting late," line to fend him off. P.S. I'm not married.

*

DAD, WE TOUCH AGAIN
By Sharon Gee

For my father, Donald E. Gee 1931 - 1976 (Thanksgiving)

I was thirteen when the ambulance came.
Moments before, you mixed a White Russian, heavy cream.
Also the way you liked your coffee.

I can still see the bar glass on the coffee table,
Emptied two or three sips
Just below the wedding-engraved initials.

I see mom's frightened look,
A stained glass window of a woman,
Dialing the telephone, EMERGENCY!

She searches my father's eyes
From the kitchen doorway
As if her gaze holds his life steady.

He meets her stare, half smiling,
Then turns his gaze to me and finishes his smile
Almost playful, with a wink.
I think I smiled back.

Funny how the fire trucks arrived first,
You would later say to me.
How you heard the sirens, you would swear,
Before you had ended the call.

I heard them too, mom.
I can still hear them
Even now as I pour this White Russian, heavy cream
Just below the rim of my uncut glass.

CHAPTER TEN

Job Bloopers

A life spent making mistakes is not only more honorable, but more useful than a life spent doing nothing. -GEORGE BERNARD SHAW

All well-oiled machines can throw a gear, and sometimes even the most sacred of moments can go wrong. In the funeral industry, there is no shortage of tales to tell about the day when something happened at the worst possible time. Have you ever experienced a blooper or a day when nothing went right?

*

STEPHEN BARON
Stephen is a 64-year-old funeral service
licensee in Grand Haven, Michigan

Even the best maintained equipment will offer up a surprise from time to time and usually does, as it did one warm, sunny spring morning for us. Our staff was working a funeral at one of the local Roman Catholic churches. We often served families in this parish and were very familiar with the church staff, as were they with us. This particular funeral was for a local city government politician and was very well attended. It seemed as though everyone we knew was in attendance. Officials from neighboring cities and townships, state and county officials, leaders in the business and retail community, and many church and school administrators and employees were there.

Our staff was well represented, some of whom had canceled days off because we simply needed the staff on this and other services scheduled for that day. We had made arrangements to have our newest funeral coach, which was stationed at our location on the other side of the city, to be used on this funeral and we had limousines borrowed from other firms to supplement our own fleet. We were looking very good as always.

Our staff had configured an extremely long procession of cars. We engaged law enforcement agencies along our route for both escort and to block major intersections enroute to the Diocesan Cemetery located some seven or so miles away. We exited the church with as much pomp as I had ever seen. The pallbearers placed the casket in the waiting hearse, the bishop said a departing prayer, and the family was ushered to the waiting limousines.

We waited for the signal from our parking staff indicating that everyone was in their automobiles and we were cleared to pull out onto the main road. The local police had taken their position in front of our lead car. Two other officers pulled their patrol vehicles in place to block through traffic. The escorting officer pulled his car out of the drive and onto the road. I put the gear selector in drive and felt the hearse drop down the driveway approach onto the road where it did not respond to my pressing on the accelerator. I went absolutely nowhere. The police and our lead car were by now a city block down the road before they noticed that the rest of the procession had not come with them.

I sat there for what seemed to be an eternity (but in actuality was only seconds) when several of our staff came into the roadway to my rescue. One of our men ordered me to release the hood and he quickly opened it and seemed to crawl inside. He briefly looked inside, stood up, closed the hood and said, "Go, go, go!" I again put the car in drive and was off. I had not a clue what had happened or what went on to fix it. All I knew is that we were moving and I was catching up to our lead car.

Later that day, after I came from another service, I saw that young man and asked him what had happened and just what he had done to save us from total embarrassment in front of all those fine people. He explained it to me this way. Apparently, what attached the gear selector to the transmission was what amounted to not much more than a cotter key type of device. It had snapped off and he had experienced this before. He replaced it with a large paperclip he had in his pocket, and it worked.

Later that same day, after two more services and trips to the cemetery, that hearse was taken to the dealership and repaired. Imagine...an eighty thousand dollar car, made operational by a simple paperclip.

*

CHASTIN BRINKLEY
Chastin is a 47-year-old funeral director, embalmer
and cremation specialist in Buckley, Washington

One of the worst days I had was with the first funeral home I worked for. I had just left a cemetery across town and traffic was at a crawl. Eventually, the congestion lifted a bit and the traffic started moving at normal speeds. The air conditioner was on its coldest setting and I remember seeing my breath when I exhaled. So I went to adjust the temperature settings. After making my adjustments, I looked up and the car in front of me was stopped. I slammed on the brakes but it was too late. Not only did I hit the car in front of me, I caused the person I hit to hit two more cars! I was mortified! Luckily, no one needed medical attention.

As we were waiting for the police to arrive, a news helicopter started circling. I immediately went and took the funeral home name plates out of the windows. When I arrived back at the funeral home I had to go face the owners. They were in the upstairs office having a family meeting. I was crying and scared, not only about losing my job, but also about losing the apartment the funeral home provided. The owner's daughter asked me, "What's wrong?"

I said, "I'm sorry."

She asked again, "Chastin, what's wrong?"

I replied, "I'm sorry."

She then asked, "Chastin, what did you do?"

I barely got out, "I was in the coach and hit three cars in front of me!"

She asked if anyone was hurt and I told her no. She then said, "That is what insurance is for," and sent me home for the rest of the day. I was very appreciative of her graciousness.

*

LAUREN BUDROW
Lauren is a 44-year-old funeral director
and funeral service educator

Fortunately, I have never had a flat tire in a procession. I did have a situation when I received a phone call from my removal crew telling me they did not have the person in the preparation room they were supposed to have picked up from the airport. About that time, I received a call from a funeral home an hour north who coincidentally was looking for the very person my removal team had in our possession. They had the person I was looking for in their custody. The airport crew had switched the containers and given each funeral home the other's deceased person. We were able to correct the situation in plenty of time and avoid a much larger problem.

*

JASON RYAN ENGLER
Jason is a 36-year-old funeral director, certified celebrant,
and cremation historian in Rogers, Arkansas

I recall an experience when I was caring for some folks who had become friends. Upon arrival at the cemetery, the positioning of the casket on the lowering device made the backdrop our funeral home's hearse. It was a hazy day, so I left the parking lights on to illuminate the coach lamps on the side of our hearse. I felt this helped make the hearse a bit more presentable as a backdrop. And it did. Unfortunately, this also drained the hearse's battery. It was on a single-car lane of the cemetery, and all the cars were lined up behind me. When I got in the hearse to move it, the key turned and clicked. Those friends still like to recall the story whenever I am with them!

*

SHARON GEE-MASCARELLO
Sharon is a 53-year-old funeral director and embalming instructor
in the Mortuary Science Program at Wayne State University in Detroit

Domino days. When one thing goes south and leads to another and to another. Set alarm for p.m. versus a.m., subsequently overslept, late for work, forgot lunch, sprayed my new suit with super glue while doing a last minute touch-up in the visitation room. Worked funeral in "white spotted" suit feeling that all eyes were upon me, ran nylons carrying the jack stands, more eyes upon me. At graveside, wire cable snapped during vault lowering, family screamed with laughter. Unexpected response. My nonpoker face was put to the test. Family shared that Grandpa was the "king of things gone wrong" and this was his final display. He also loved more than anything to make his grandchildren laugh. He got his wish!

*

LOUISE GOHMANN
Louise is a 61-year-old mortuary school educator
and funeral director in Jeffersonville, Indiana

Burying someone in the wrong place is a funeral director's worst nightmare. The cemetery where I worked had a very elaborate flag system to prevent wrongful burials. First a red flag identified the grave, then a pink flag was placed by a family member showing that they agreed that it was the correct space. Finally, a third person with a yellow flag did a blind check to be absolutely sure. On this particular day, a grave was flagged, the family member flagged, and the blind checker decided to save time and put the final flag out before he went home for the evening.

We had a new landscaping crew come in that evening to mow. The mower operator ran over the flags and couldn't figure out where they went, so he just stuck them on another grave. The next morning, the gravedigger came, and seeing the flags, went to work digging the grave. An hour before the service, the vault man showed up with the burial vault. He immediately called and told us to stop, we were about to bury this man in the wrong grave. The reason he knew that it was the wrong grave was because the deceased was his neighbor, and he had buried his wife the year before, and her grave was about twenty feet from this one!

I thanked him profusely, and have done so every time I've seen him over the years.

*

KAREN JELLY
Karen is a 44-year-old funeral director
and mortician in Havre, Montana

We really haven't had equipment break down at an inopportune moment. However, I have had more days when everything went wrong than I can count. These include days when the minister for the service contracted the flu overnight, the ground was too frozen to dig the grave to bury, the pianist was in a car accident the day before the service, the vocalist got laryngitis, and any other number of calamities. Sometimes, those days just include feeling like everything I try to do turns out completely the opposite of the intended result. However, those days are few and far between, and usually caused by too much work and too little sleep for several days. Work smooths out, and everything seems right again.

*

CODY JONES
Cody is a 37-year-old progressive funeral home owner
and funeral director in Bryan-College Station, Texas

Our hearse did stall out one time on the way to set up for a church funeral. Thankfully this was not in a funeral procession as we were just on our way to the church. We were able to unload the casket into a different vehicle and continue to the church. After having the hearse towed, we learned that someone had poured bleach into the gas tank.

*

CORIANN MARTIN
Coriann is a 42-year-old funeral director
and embalmer in Kenosha, Wisconsin

I have to knock on wood that equipment malfunction has not yet happened to me. If you count weak pallbearers almost dropping a casket, then I've been there before.

I have, however, made the occasional mistake. I made a wrong turn going to the cemetery and had to have the whole procession make a u-turn. While driving in procession, I reached a railroad crossing and noticed a train was coming but the arm hadn't started to lower yet. I was already too close to the tracks, and the arm came down on the roof of the lead car. I needed to back up, causing the crossing arm to scrape all the way down the roof to the windshield before landing on the hood of the car.

No funeral is ever perfect. I do my best to be at my best, but sometimes you can't help but find the humor in it all.

*

SHAWNA RODABAUGH
Shawna is a 37-year-old funeral director and
embalmer in Mount Pleasant, Michigan

We had been extremely busy one week at work, and I had barely slept. One of our other directors had met with a family to arrange the funeral, but I was the director who was going to run the funeral. I went through everything in the file, and thought everything had been set, but the morning of the funeral, I realized that I had neglected to call the cemetery to have the grave opened, or to order the vault for the casket. I have never felt so sick in my life. I called the cemetery and had the chapel set aside for a service, and we ended up doing the burial the next day when the cemetery was able to open the grave. The family was more understanding than I would have been in that circumstance, and I never forgot that feeling.

*

STEVE TWEEDLE
Steve is a 42-year-old funeral
director in Ocala, Florida

The worst day I had was the day there was a crash at the local racetrack. The two drivers who were involved in the accident were killed. We were called by one of the families to take their decedent into our care, proceed with the embalming, and send the deceased up north for services.

The brother of the decedent was dispatched by the family to come down to Florida to oversee everything. He was a super nice guy. During the arrangements, he asked me if he could see his brother before we sent him up north. I told him that there would not be an issue with that and we set up a time for him to come back. He explained that through the years he and his brother had grown apart and he needed some time with him before they got up north.

We placed his brother into a container called a combination unit, which is a minimum container required by the airlines that we use for transferring people via common carrier. These containers are used when a family chooses to buy a casket in their hometown rather than locally. When he came in, I brought him back to the private viewing area. After a few minutes he came out and I asked if everything was okay. I had expected him to be in there longer given the history he had told me about. He said to me, "Let me preface everything I'm about to say by telling you this. I haven't seen my brother in a long, long time, but I don't think that's him." Let me tell you, I puckered in places I didn't know I could pucker.

Needless to say this is a funeral director's worst nightmare. We train our staff to check every piece of identification they can get their hands on. They look at ankle bracelets and wristbands. My mind immediately started racing. How could this happen? Who made the removal? Was there an ankle bracelet? Obviously, as professionals we try to ease the burden people go through—not add to it. And then I said the three words I wish I could take back. I can't think of anything I can regret saying to a family more than this. "Are you kidding?"

For me it was an out of body experience. I was watching myself talk to this person, like I was watching a funeral director talk to a family on a bad television show. Besides the potential legal ramifications of what happened, I just added to the trauma. I made this harder on this family than I needed to. As mentioned earlier, we try to lessen a burden, and I just added to it.

The brother took a second to process my question. "No, I'm not kidding. I'm pretty sure that's not my brother." As I began to come to my senses, we walked over to the combination unit and I read the ankle bracelet secured by the hospital. Sure enough, it read correctly. I showed it to the brother.

"I see it says my brother's name, but it's not him."

Then it occurred to me that two people were involved in the accident. Is it possible the first responders got the two confused? I explained to the brother what I thought had occurred. We called the hospital and found out that the second victim had been released to a funeral home about an hour away. I called and explained to that funeral director what was going on.

"I'm glad you called me. The person we have here is scheduled to be cremated soon," he said.

I offered to jump in the car with our deceased victim and drive to the other funeral home to switch bodies. The family member who was with me said, "No. I want to drive to that funeral home and see the person who's there. I told you I hadn't seen my brother in a long time and I want to make sure that he is at that funeral home."

About an hour later I got a phone call that we needed to come to their funeral home and bring the correct person under our care. As the days went on we discovered that the first responders had in fact gotten them confused. In the chaos of trying to pull both victims out of the racecars to treat them on scene, they had gotten mislabeled. I couldn't imagine the responsibility and the weight the first responders were dealing with in that situation.

*

BRIAN VAN HECK
Brian is a 41-year-old funeral director in
the Lake Norman area of North Carolina

I have often equated what we, as funeral directors, do to what a bride does to plan her wedding. The major difference is that a bride takes a year to plan everything to pull off her major life event, whereas we do the same in about three days. We secure a venue, arrange for appropriate transportation and clergy or other celebrant to officiate the ceremony, and typically arrange a meal or reception after the ceremony itself. Just as a bride stresses about everything going off without a glitch the day of her wedding, so do I the day of a service. After all, we only get one opportunity to give this family the perfect service for their loved one. There might be little items that don't always go perfectly, but we can make the necessary adjustments as long as we don't panic. Other times, no adjustments can be made and we have a situation on our hands, but hopefully not a crisis.

One such story happened after an 11 a.m. funeral at a church. We had a full procession of vehicles lined up ready to make our way to the cemetery for the interment. The family was secure in the limousine, and the casket had been placed in the hearse. The minister was in the passenger seat of my lead car when I gave the nod to the hearse and limo driver. The hearse driver realized the door was locked with the keys in it. Knowing the spare set of keys was back at the funeral home twenty minutes away, that was not the best option. I told the family what was going on. Fortunately, they were able to find humor in the situation rather than anger. Our best option was to take the casket out of the hearse, crawl through the back and reach through to the driver's seat to obtain the key and unlock the door. It was an embarrassing moment but certainly could have been worse. About ten minutes later, we were under way to the cemetery.

*

KIMBERLY VARELA
Kimberly is a 41-year-old funeral director
and embalmer in Westland, Michigan

I was removing a rental unit from the casket shell when the church truck sprung a bolt and collapsed under the weight. Luckily, the deceased was safely tucked into the crematable container and suffered no injury, but due to their size, I was faced with how to safely raise the container off the floor and onto a church truck. I had never apologized as much as I did to that poor decedent. Through sheer determination, luck and paying attention in physics class, I was able to rig a harness using straps and an oversize body mover to our lift and raise the container, deceased and all. What was supposed to be fifteen minutes of work turned into a few hours of sweat, tears and a valuable lesson, all over a tiny bolt.

*

DAN WELCH
Dan is a 30-year-old funeral director and
embalmer in Wichita, Kansas

Thankfully I have only had one catastrophic equipment failure in my career. It took place when I was an apprentice in mortuary school while working for a removal service. I was dispatched on a call to a hospital where I was quickly presented with a decedent who weighed nearly five hundred pounds.

After about thirty minutes of maneuvering with various nurses and a security guard, we were finally able to get the decedent on the cot. As we rolled the cot down the hall toward the elevator, I quickly realized the elevator was right in front of the waiting room. With me on one end of the cot, I had a nurse on each side and the security guard on the other side. As we began to enter the elevator, the first set of wheels became lodged in the threshold of the elevator doors.

Knowing that we had an entire audience with the waiting room directly in front of us, the security guard, thinking he was helping, grabbed underneath the cot and began to pull. Unfortunately, what he had grabbed was one of the release handles to the cot. Due to the sheer weight on the cot, just dropping down the one notch caused the entire cot to spontaneously crumble upon itself, causing parts of the cot to shoot as far as fifteen feet in every direction, and the body plummeting to the floor.

Never have I wanted to disappear more than in that moment. Thankfully, I had a second cot in the van and after multiple good samaritans and a couple emergency medical technicians who helped, I was able to successfully take the decedent into my care. Never again do I want to experience that, nor would I wish that on my worst enemy.

*

LIGHTING THE CANDLE

By Sharon Gee

For my uncle, Richard Floyd 1938-1986
My uncle died by suicide while I was in
mortuary school. His was my first cremation.

My heart does not stop, but suffers this rend

And surges beyond, not quickly to mend.

Too heavy with loss, too sudden to grieve,

Family and friends for strength on this eve.

I am the youngest, my flame flickers least

As morning sun breathes steady first from the east.

Sets fire among us, warming now four,

We scream for the fifth, pound strongly once more!

I stand with your picture, your lips held still,

My eyes wide and searching, fearful until

I am drawn from your gaze, always so kind

To the soft hush of candles warm in my mind.

And gentle within me an answering breath

Dances the red ember song of your death.

*

CHAPTER ELEVEN

Unusual Requests

The greatness of art is not to find what is common
but what is unique. -ISAAC BASHEVIS SINGER

While traditional services are tried and true, more and more families are looking for something different when it comes to memorializing their loved one. Whether it be a celebration of life, a green burial, or designing a treasure hunt that takes mourners on a tour of locations that were meaningful to the deceased, the possibilities are endless. What has been the most unique service you've planned?

*

STEPHEN BARON
Stephen is a 64-year-old funeral service
licensee in Grand Haven, Michigan

Years ago, a family made an appointment to come in to talk about funeral arrangements for their father who was very close to death. During that phone conversation, they said the same thing that many families say. That was that they had never made funeral arrangements before and that they would come with many questions about what could and should be done and what was proper. I assured them that having this conversation prior to their dad's death would more than likely prove beneficial and would give them some time to process their findings and make decisions. In closing, the daughter said that they may have some unusual requests and asked if that was okay. I told her that they could be comfortable asking me their questions.

When they came in the next day, I could tell they were nervous, but at the same time there was something that told me that they were well adjusted and very realistic. Their requests were centered around a part of their father's life that was very important to him and was, from my perspective, the reason the family appeared to be in a sound emotional position. Dad was an amateur clown. While away in military service during WWII, he saw a clown performing for children who were frightened and alone after bombings in a European city. He decided then that children need and deserve laughter in their lives. Starting with an early birthday party for his oldest child soon after he returned from the war, he started to offer his clowning abilities to others and as a result, "Crackers the Clown" was born.

What I remember most about the funeral service was the fact that children and young people outnumbered his peers. Many of those in attendance were now adults, who as children, attended events where Crackers was the featured entertainment. The service was held at a park where he had often entertained children over the years. There were many other clowns attending and a majority of the other people who came were honoring the family's request that guests come in face paint. There was a clown band and a calliope that played as guests arrived and there was popcorn, hotdogs and cotton candy for everyone. During the service, a clown juggling act featured and many speakers and clowns made everyone laugh. In addition to all the fun, frolic and secular parts of the service, there was a twenty-minute Christian worship service under the auspices of two congregational pastors from the church where Cracker was a longtime member. After the service at the park, the family and close friends gathered at the family part in a local cemetery where the casket and body were interred and Military Honors were conducted.

I have had two funerals of clowns since, but the first was an excellent example of good planning on the family's behalf. I learned from working with that family that a funeral service can salute many facets of a life lived and be meaningful on all counts, if the family and participants work and plan together.

*

CHASTIN BRINKLEY
Chastin is a 47-year-old funeral director, embalmer
and cremation specialist in Buckley, Washington

One of the most unique services in which I was involved was arranged by a coworker. The memorial service was for a man who loved Hawaii and was a football player. It was held at a local community center adjacent to a football field. The funeral home staff and ushers all wore colorful Hawaiian shirts provided by the family. The decedent was cremated and, after unlacing the football, I placed his cremated remains inside. For his great sendoff, all in attendance walked outside to the football field, where his family and friends took turns running the football up and down the field.

Another memorable service I arranged was for a young lady who was mentally and physically challenged. During the arrangement conference, the girl's parents mentioned how she looked forward to seeing big dump trucks drive by their house. They lived next to a dump truck business. When the truck drivers' shift was over, they would drive by her house and her face would light up as she would say, "Truck! Truck!" She liked the vibration the trucks gave off as she could feel it on her chest.

On the day of her funeral, I arrived at the church early to set up flowers and the guest book. Then, at just the right time, I asked her family, along with the minister, to come outside. They followed me outside. As they looked across the parking lot at the stop light, they saw a big dump truck. Behind it was our funeral coach. They said it was an appropriate coincidence. Then they saw another dump truck pull up to the light behind our coach. It wasn't until they all made a left turn toward the church that her mom and dad realized the trucks were escorting their daughter. Emotion took over those in the parking lot and there wasn't a dry eye to be found. Her parents hugged both of the drivers and invited them to stay for the service, which they did. I was thankful that the trucking company was able to take two of their trucks out of service to honor this young lady.

*

LAUREN BUDROW
Lauren is a 44-year-old funeral director
and funeral service educator

I feel quite fortunate to have had a variety of funeral services in my career. It is difficult, if not impossible, to say which one was more unique than all the others. Each funeral or memorial service is unique by nature of the fact that the impressions people leave on each other's lives is like an individual fingerprint. I approached every funeral arrangement and service with the same intention to carry out all details, even the mundane, with great care. Some of those services were simply more work than others but not done with any less care.

Some of my most memorable have been the military or public service organizations. My only riderless horse and caisson funeral occurred when I was still an intern, and it was for a retired general. It was the most planning, pomp and circumstance I had seen for a service at the time. The army met us at the cemetery gates and I pulled over to let the military take over. I wasn't sure if I was directing or watching at that point. I wanted to stop and observe everything but still had to stay in my professional role. As a new funeral director, it was awe-inspiring and intimidating to be part of.

I have had the honor of being the director for four active duty military deaths: two marines, one navy, one army. Each branch of service has its own unique way of handling the funeral arrangement and service. They are all a bit stressful to coordinate, but are always impressive. The police and firefighter services are similar in that way as well. The most challenging aspect is managing the large number of attendees. It's not only the people, but the seating and the cars and the needs of hundreds of people in one event while being *the* funeral director. For example, I was the funeral director for a child who accidentally got tangled in the window blinds and suffocated. His parents were members of the police department, and his funeral was the largest gathering of officers I had ever seen in one room—over six hundred officers and support members. The procession had so many motorcycle officers surrounding the coach, I was terrified I would hit one with the car. These people weren't at the funeral for the child, they were there to support the family. It was an incredible outpouring of support I had never before seen on such a scale.

*

JASON RYAN ENGLER
Jason is a 36-year-old funeral director, certified celebrant,
and cremation historian in Rogers, Arkansas

The most unique service I've ever been part of was the service of our state's lieutenant governor. While I wasn't responsible for the service, I was assigned to lead the transportation of the lieutenant governor's spouse and family for his lying in state at the capitol rotunda, private family session with the House of Representatives, flyover on the steps of the state capitol, and for the service the following day. I was also responsible for directing the seating of a former American president who was in attendance, and afterward for ceremoniously carrying his urn out of the church at the conclusion of the service. It is a memory I will not soon forget!

*

SHARON GEE-MASCARELLO

Sharon is a 53-year-old funeral director and embalming instructor
in the Mortuary Science Program at Wayne State University in Detroit

A gentleman's lifelong desire to travel the world, having lost both his legs, was realized after his cremation. Sometimes the planning of a personal and unique funeral is Faulkneresque; the director and family stream thoughts, unedited, and the result is perfection.

The gentleman and his wife were both pharmacists. A wicker basket containing a hundred prescription bottles were filled with a symbolic amount of his cremated remains and attached to a postcard perched next to the guest register. Each guest signed in and received a vial. During the funeral, his wife made a plea: "My husband wanted to travel the world. Please take his ashes along on your next trip. Scatter them and record the location on the postcard." One year later, the postcards were read at an anniversary memorial. Oh, the places he did go! Mountain climbing, scuba diving, wild game hunting. And the music he made, too. He actually became one with a set of maracas, keeping rhythm on a CD!

*

LOUISE GOHMANN

Louise is a 61-year-old mortuary school educator
and funeral director in Jeffersonville, Indiana

The most unique service I ever helped plan was my sister's. I think if he could have, her doctor would have listed her cause of death as stubbornness. She knew more than all the doctors, and as a result, she died from ignoring their instructions and neglecting her health.

My sister had been a stand-up comic in her younger years, and swore that when she died she wanted to wear a red clown nose so she could make people laugh one last time. Her children were well aware of her wish, and when we were making the arrangements I said, "You know what we have to do, right?"

The day of her service happened to fall on the very first Red Nose Day in the United States. Coincidence? I think not. We went all out. If she was going to wear a clown nose, we all were. As people arrived for the service, the ushers handed each person a program and a red nose. Wearing a red nose, the minister led the procession to Frank Sinatra singing "My Way." It was the most appropriate song we could think of.

*

KAREN JELLY
Karen is a 44-year-old funeral director
and mortician in Havre, Montana

The most unique service I helped plan was one that incorporated a woman's Native American cultural traditions and the traditions commonly found in memorial services for Caucasian individuals. She was a fairly young woman, in her mid-forties, who worked at the local university as the multicultural coordinator. She had blended both backgrounds so well in life, that her family and I wanted to honor both backgrounds in death.

During the service, congregational hymns were sung, and a Native American journey song was played and sung before the end of the service. The family wanted a time of sharing, and both Native Americans and white individuals whose lives she'd touched stood up and spoke about what a wonderful woman she was. The service lasted about two hours, which is unusual, but it was a heartfelt, emotional tribute to a woman who would have done anything to help anyone of any background continue their education.

She was a truly special woman, and thinking of her now brings tears to my eyes. I felt truly honored to be part of planning such a beautiful service, and being able to be part of that was very emotionally rewarding. Her family was very happy with the service, and while I found it to be unusual, I also felt that it was truly beautiful. I enjoyed the service immensely.

*

CORIANN MARTIN
Coriann is a 42-year-old funeral director
and embalmer in Kenosha, Wisconsin

I don't know if I would consider this the most unique funeral service I've ever planned, but it was definitely the most labor intensive funeral that we ever pulled off. A local football coach passed away in our community. He had taught countless children over the years and his family really wanted to focus on the influence he had on the local youth athletes. We brought in a set of metal bleachers, footballs and jerseys for the kids to sign. The chapel was filled with all of his awards and pictures throughout the years. It was an amazing tribute to a man who shaped the future of so many kids in our community.

*

LACY ROBINSON
Lacy is a 38-year-old Director of Member Development for the
National Funeral Directors Association in Brookfield, Wisconsin

Over the last decade visiting funeral homes across the country, I've had the opportunity to learn about the most unique services funeral directors have helped families plan. I've heard about tribute events taking place on beautiful golf courses and on stunning beaches. Most recently I spoke with a funeral director who helped a family plan a meaningful tribute for their young son. It was important to the mother and father to create a very unique casket for their son. The end result was a blue and red Superman themed casket with their son's name painted in bright yellow.

I've always appreciated funeral directors who approach every service as telling the life story of a family's loved one. A funeral director emailed pictures of a visitation for a gentleman who played in a polka band, participated in civil war reenactments, and spent his free time at the Jersey Shore. The funeral director and family set up scenes throughout the funeral home that depicted those different interests using the deceased's belongings. There were also high top tables and refreshments available, which allowed guests to visit with one another in a very relaxed environment that encouraged everyone to share memories and stories.

Funeral directors have also shared with me how they have helped family and friends participate in a unique way. They've sent me pictures of caskets where every guest in attendance wrote a special sentiment on it. I've heard about remarkable funeral processions that included fifty tow trucks or had a vintage car leading the procession.

One service in particular I remember hearing about included the high school cross country team leading the procession wearing special shirts honoring their coach who had died unexpectedly. Another service I'll never forget was for a gentleman who died in a tragic plane crash. At the conclusion of the committal service, each family member took a long stem rose from a vase and placed it on the casket. It was a very meaningful way for the immediate family to participate and for everyone observing, it was truly a very profound moment.

*

SHAWNA RODABAUGH
Shawna is a 37-year-old funeral director and
embalmer in Mount Pleasant, Michigan

The most unique service I've planned was a home service for a young woman who had passed unexpectedly. Although services out of the family's home used to be the way every service was conducted, in recent history, the majority of the services are conducted out of the funeral home or church, just for space considerations. Planning everything, from our ability to get the casket in and out of the doorways, to directing traffic around the residence, was a challenge.

In the end though, it gave the family a sense of comfort to have her in the home, and that's what we are here to provide.

*

STEVE TWEEDLE
Steve is a 42-year-old funeral
director in Ocala, Florida

I had a family tell me that they took their mom to the doctor at ninety years of age. The doctor examined their mom, came back and said she needed to cut down on her cholesterol. The daughter told me she was thinking about what the doctor had said while driving home. The more she thought about it, the angrier she got.

She told her mom, "Mom, you're ninety years old. If you want to eat eggs, you can eat 'em!"

She then told me that every Sunday she went to her mom's house, cooked her eggs, and they watched the Three Tenors together, her mom's favorite group. She told me that she was going to miss their Sunday mornings. I suggested that we have the funeral on Sunday, and that she bring the Three Tenors DVD that they watched. I then enlisted one of our part-time guys who was an active Mason. Whenever the Masons had an event that required cooking, he was the cook. After the funeral, we played the Three Tenors for everyone and cooked eggs for all of those in attendance. She got to have that experience one more time with her mom.

I met with a lady one time who had lost her husband. They were young, in their late forties or early fifties, from what I can remember. They had never had children, but what they did for fun was travel around and listen to bands. They had seen several famous people in concert, but what they loved most was live local bands that played the blues. One of the guys that worked for me happened to be a drummer in a band. As I was walking out of the arrangement office, he was coming down the hall. It was very much a Blues Brothers moment. I looked at him and said, "We're getting the band back together!" He called his buddies, and when the family came in for their first view, they started playing their favorite song.

I met a woman who lost her daughter to an overdose. Although the decedent was in her early twenties, it was as though the mother had lost her twelve-year-old daughter. It seemed like the mother had already lost the person who was in the casket, so we were having a funeral for the daughter she remembered before the drugs. She kept talking about when the decedent was younger and how she was on her way to becoming an accomplished horse rider. She spoke as if the little girl was still with her and had not aged into the person she was.

I called a local therapeutic riding association and asked if they had a horse we could use. I wanted the horse to be in the front yard for people to pet. The night of the visitation, the horse arrived. Without the mother knowing, we moved it to the front of the building. After the horse was set up, I asked the mother to come outside and told her I needed to show her something. We opened the door and there was Barney, a retired police horse standing tall and proud. The mother immediately began crying and threw her arms around me. She thanked me over and over. She spent the first hour of the time she was there talking to that horse. What was said was between her and that horse, but hopefully we helped her to begin the healing process.

These are the things that are important and that we have to be ready to coordinate. The funeral director must be ready, and be bold enough to suggest ideas that are meaningful. I felt a sense of accomplishment, and pride. These aren't easy things to do. But to see the family react and to know that you are helping them makes it worth all the pain we see.

*

BRIAN VAN HECK
Brian is a 41-year-old funeral director in
the Lake Norman area of North Carolina

Jill was thirty-seven years old. Her family thought she would be coming home from the hospital a few days after a routine procedure and treatment. Instead, she developed an infection. Two weeks later, the day after Jill's death, her family was sitting with me talking about her arrangements.

We spent a great deal of time talking about what they wanted, and how they wanted to honor Jill's life. Her parents and two sisters shared that they did not want to cremate Jill, but felt like that was their only option. They didn't have a grave or even know where they wanted to bury her. This was an opportunity for me to educate them that they had the option to have a service for Jill in the immediate future, and still take time to select and obtain a proper final resting place for Jill. The amount of relief and comfort that overcame them with that permission was tremendous.

With that roadblock removed, we went on to arrange one of the most personalized and unique services I have been a part of. It was Christmas time; Jill loved Christmas and her favorite color was red. Armed with that information, I began making suggestions to the family. We scheduled an evening service so that her coworkers could attend but also so we could have a candlelight service (red candles of course). Her casket was blanketed with evergreens and red roses, and musical selections included a congregational singing of "Silent Night." We compiled a video tribute to Jill with all of her favorite music (that CD often makes its way into my player because it is so good and I always think of Jill when I listen to it). The funeral home Christmas tree was positioned near the entrance to the chapel. We decided to remove all of our ornaments and replace them with red Glad ornaments that we had artfully written Jill's name on. As each guest of Jill's family left that evening, they received a keepsake ornament.

The family still had not decided upon her final resting place. The above mentioned service took place and the family was well pleased. I told Jill's parents to get through the next days and weeks of Christmas and move at their pace to search for cemetery property. A week or so after Christmas, Jill's father called and told me they had purchased graves about three hours away near where one of her sisters lived. So, a few weeks after we honored Jill with that evening candlelight service, the family gathered at the cemetery to lay Jill to rest. Through this journey with Jill's family we became very close and still stay in touch from time to time.

So much of what I do as a funeral director is listening and suggesting ideas. Not every family likes my ideas or wants the suggestions I make but I owe it to them and their loved one to offer because grief often takes away their ability to think clearly. They need the gentle, loving, guiding hand of the funeral director.

*

KIMBERLY VARELA
Kimberly is a 41-year-old funeral director
and embalmer in Westland, Michigan

A family had requested a funeral service centered around the band Insane Clown Posse. For those unaware, Google it. Not exactly funeral appropriate but when in Rome... Needless to say, the crowd was young, rowdy and came fully decked out in juggalo face paint and clothing. Insane Clown Posse songs blasted through the funeral home and parking lot. The fact that I have a phobia of clowns made for a long night. At the end, when I came to the front of the room for announcements and dismissal, you could hear a pin drop. A packed chapel of painted faces looked at me unwaveringly as I talked about what they taught me about their loved one and what I hoped they would remember about him. Everyone filed past the casket with reverence and every attendee shook my hand and thanked me or hugged me. It was a sweet gesture but I could have done without being hugged by seventy-five or so clowns. My nerves were a wreck!

The family closed with me and as I readied him for the crematory the next morning, I found a huge stash of joints tucked in just about every corner of the casket. The rental had to be aired out for a few days because of it and I had to alert the crematory staff about the possible contact high.

*

DAN WELCH
Dan is a 30-year-old funeral director and
embalmer in Wichita, Kansas

Early in my funeral career I had the opportunity to assist in arranging a funeral for a man who had created and owned a very large theme park within the area. The man was very well known and liked by everyone. The family had indicated that they wanted to incorporate his love and passion for the theme park into the service. The entire day leading up to the visitation and funeral we had multiple staff members and members of the family convert our chapel and funeral home to look and feel like the theme park he had owned and created. From top to bottom and front to back, the funeral home was converted over. We had everything from a bumper car to skee-ball to a carousel horse. There were games for the kids and entertainment for the adults. The music was the same music he played at the theme park and in order to get into the service everyone was given an actual admission ticket from the theme park he owned. In my short career as a funeral professional it was by far one of my favorite services to have been a part of and truly set the standard for a celebration of life service in my opinion.

*

A funeral is not a day in a lifetime.
It is a lifetime in a day.

UNKNOWN

*

CHAPTER TWELVE

STRANGE Last Rites

It's a strange world. Let's keep it that way.
-WARREN ELLIS

Unusual last rites range from banning black clothing and partying with the deceased propped in the recliner, to hiring professional funeral clowns to put the fun back in funeral. As a funeral director, what was the strangest request you've received thus far?

*

STEPHEN BARON
Stephen is a 64-year-old funeral service
licensee in Grand Haven, Michigan

I have buried and cremated people with every conceivable object that will fit inside a casket. What I thought strange in the early part of my career, now, in many cases, no longer seems all that strange. I've had requests for golf clubs, musical instruments, garden tools, construction tools, extra clothing, suitcases, Scotch whisky, bourbon, beer, soda pop, sporting goods, kitchen utensils, auto parts, photos of grandchildren, photos of the spouse, photos of past or current lovers, pet cremains, human cremains and the little black book. You name it!

Not the strangest but certainly one of the more memorable requests was when a member of a group of lifelong male friends died. These guys had played poker together for over fifty years. The surviving friends were asked to be pallbearers and they were all to be present at the closing of the casket following the family's final viewing. The deceased was a longtime smoker and was very fond of Pall Malls. In fact, it was smoking that led to his death, but that was not to stop one of the gentlemen from stopping me while closing the casket to honor an old request of the deceased, that he be sent off with at least one pack of the smokes. I obliged. Then as I was once again attempting to close, another voice chimed in, chastising the group and saying, "You can't do that!" He quickly lifted the lid and threw in about a half dozen books of matches.

When receiving strange requests, I always tell people that as long as their request is legal, ethical and non-offensive, we will do all we can to honor the request.

*

CHASTIN BRINKLEY
Chastin is a 47-year-old funeral director, embalmer
and cremation specialist in Buckley, Washington

Strange is a subjective word. The first time I heard Guns N' Roses played at a funeral, I thought it was strange. Now it is normal to play the deceased's favorite band. I have had families request for the deceased to be delivered back to their home for viewing, for the deceased to be transferred to the cemetery in his own truck, and to place pet urns in the casket.

Once, we had a family ask attendees to wear overalls to a service to pay tribute to their father. There must have been thirty or more in overalls. It was quite a sight. Another time we had a procession from the church to the cemetery with over twenty John Deer tractors leading the procession. I believe no matter how strange the request, as long as it is legal and ethical, we should accommodate the request. By doing so, we are allowing the family to honor their loved one in a unique manner.

*

LAUREN BUDROW
Lauren is a 44-year-old funeral director
and funeral service educator

The most unusual moment was when a family had a professional photographer take family photos with their deceased baby. The family had us rearrange furniture so the photographer could get different settings. The pictures were not my biggest concern though. It was the passing back and forth of the deceased infant that worried me. This was a very tiny, premature infant and the family was having even their two-year-old son hold her for pictures. This was not a doll and I began to feel protective of the baby. I didn't want to leave the chapel because I wanted to make sure the deceased infant was being handled carefully by her family, but being in the room watching it was bothersome to me. It was a strange twist of roles. I felt as if I was the caretaker of that baby now, and knew how to best care for her now that she was dead.

*

JASON RYAN ENGLER
Jason is a 36-year-old funeral director, certified celebrant,
and cremation historian in Rogers, Arkansas

This may sound like an overly diplomatic answer, but I don't consider any request too strange. When I was a high school student, the funeral home where I worked dressed a lady in her wedding dress and the husband renewed his vows to her during her funeral. I did find that a bit different.

*

SHARON GEE-MASCARELLO
Sharon is a 53-year-old funeral director and embalming instructor
in the Mortuary Science Program at Wayne State University in Detroit

A colleague who was having a very bad day implored me to place her upside down and naked in her casket so that everyone who walked by could kiss her @#&! I asked her to record her request in a preplanning guide. She did. That way, I didn't have to disagree.

*

LOUISE GOHMANN
Louise is a 61-year-old mortuary school educator
and funeral director in Jeffersonville, Indiana

The list of strange requests is endless. One daughter said her mom's favorite song was "Oh, Dem Golden Slippers," and asked us to find gold shoes for her to wear in heaven. We did, and I like to think she is dancing in heaven today in her golden slippers. My favorite was, "Mom never went anywhere without her purse and her cellphone." We made sure that Mom went to eternity with those treasured items.

*

KAREN JELLY
Karen is a 44-year-old funeral director
and mortician in Havre, Montana

I have experienced many unusual requests over the years; every funeral director will if they work in this industry long enough. Most of mine run the gamut of asking to put cigarettes or beer in the casket (sometimes they don't ask, and I don't tell), writing on the casket of a young person in Sharpie (giving their friends a chance to say goodbye), branding a wooden casket with the deceased's brand, or placing a beloved pet's cremated remains in with the deceased owner. In each of these many instances, I have been happy to accommodate the requests. I believe these family members are providing their deceased loved ones with the care they would have wanted.

The only requests I would have to decline would be those which violate ethics or the law. I am a firm believer that the laws are in place for a reason, and I will stand firm in upholding them.

*

CORIANN MARTIN
Coriann is a 42-year-old funeral director
and embalmer in Kenosha, Wisconsin

One gentleman came in to plan a funeral for his brother. He requested we carry on the tradition of his brother's ability to pull off practical jokes. He asked that we publish an obituary stating that the funeral was going to be held at our funeral home but in reality it was at an alternate location a few blocks away. He wanted to have staff present at the door of our funeral home and when people arrived, they were to be told it was a joke and then where the funeral *really* was.

I understood the joke, but worried that due to the funeral being in the winter, people who trekked through the snow to get to the funeral home might not find it funny. It might even be offensive to some people. The brother was adamant that we try to pull this off. This is when I had to step in and give him suggestions of how to pull off the joke without offending or inconveniencing people. I suggested that we make up cards with his brother's picture on it saying, "The joke's on you," and then explain that he wanted to have the last laugh. We included the address of the actual location of his funeral and thankfully only upset a few people. The only thing that really mattered is that the family loved it and thought it was well received by most. Our job as professionals is to listen and guide people, hear what they want and make it happen.

*

SHAWNA RODABAUGH
Shawna is a 37-year-old funeral director and
embalmer in Mount Pleasant, Michigan

Honestly, I don't really consider any of the requests to be strange. Some requests are more difficult to accommodate, or are unusual, but I do everything I can to give the family what they want out of a service. There are so many different ways to grieve, and the funeral service is an expression of that. I've let pets come to the visitation to be with their owners, set up special objects that have meaning to a family, and contracted motorcycle hearses in order to do justice to the life that was lived. In any scenario, if it could be done, I did everything in my power to make sure the family got what they wanted.

*

STEVE TWEEDLE
Steve is a 42-year-old funeral
director in Ocala, Florida

The strangest request was one that I suggested, not thinking for one second they would say yes. The decedent was a huge Elvis fan. I suggested that we should see if we could get an Elvis impersonator to come perform. Sometimes when you suggest ideas, you're not thinking that they will accept. Sometimes going way out there on an idea will show the family that they have permission to do things. I proposed the idea more as a statement of, "We don't do funerals here, we do celebrations." My intent was to get them to let me play old Elvis concerts on television. I thought if I threw the impersonator idea out there, they'd say no and I'd counteroffer the television and Elvis DVDs. Well they said yes, they thought it was a great idea!

I spent the next several days trying to find an impersonator. I had several hang up on me thinking I was pranking them. I had one tell me how disrespectful I was that I would even suggest that for a funeral. I ended up finding one; it was a lot of sweat and tears but I found one. The family loved it. There aren't very many requests I would not accommodate. They would have to be illegal for me to say no.

*

BRIAN VAN HECK
Brian is a 41-year-old funeral director in
the Lake Norman area of North Carolina

My educational background includes graduate studies in counseling psychology, yet my response to my life's calling finds me in the career of being a funeral director. I have often said that I have learned more about people and psychology in my time as funeral director than a lifetime in a career in psychology. Additionally, I once thought that individuals on some of the talk shows were actors and actresses, however after nearly two decades in funeral service I no longer believe that to be true. The world is filled with a wide array of individuals that believe, behave and think differently. As a funeral director it is not my job to critique, evaluate or judge the bereaved. Granted it can prove to be challenging to maintain professional composure at certain requests.

When families select cremation as the choice of final disposition for their loved, there are certain legalities, varying from state to state, that must be followed. Furthermore, there are also certain standard procedures that take place. One such procedure occurs once the actual cremation process is complete and it is called processing the cremated remains. Processing the cremated remains typically includes removing them (large extremely brittle bone fragments) from the cremation chamber into a container and then placing them in the processing unit. The processing unit pulverizes these large bone fragments into much smaller particles that have an ash-like consistency, hence the majority of the public calls them ashes. The reality is that cremated remains are more accurately the pulverized bone fragments that are left upon completion of the cremation process.

Families elect to do any number of things with the cremated remains: bury, scatter or keep, just to name a few. One grieving wife, however, made a unique request. She was familiar with the technical procedure of cremation and did not want us to process the cremated remains, meaning she wanted the large bone fragments just as they came out of the cremation chamber. After having her sign an additional waiver and authorization, we filled three shopping style bags with her husband's cremated remains and she left satisfied with the service that we provided her. I have learned to accept unique requests and actually tell families that as long as it is not illegal, unethical or immoral, we will accommodate their requests.

*

KIMBERLY VARELA
Kimberly is a 41-year-old funeral director
and embalmer in Westland, Michigan

A gentleman walked into the funeral home and said his father had passed away. I asked what type of service he would like for his dad. His response was, "Just burn him, cause he's going to hell anyway." Evidently there was a long history of abuse and anger between the two but the son said out of respect for his father's service in the military, he would at least cremate him and take him to the National Cemetery for interment. It was a tense arrangement but in the end he was thankful for my services. I asked him if he would be attending the honors and he said, "Nope. Just going to dump him off like he did to me. He got more than he deserved from me." I admired the man's honesty.

*

CHAPTER THIRTEEN

Handling Dead Bodies

> If you look closely at a tree you'll notice it's knots
> and dead branches, just like our bodies. What we
> learn is that beauty and imperfection go together
> wonderfully. -MATTHEW FOX

Morticians clean and prepare dead bodies so family and friends can view and remember their loved one with fondness. Although death is a part of life, handling the deceased requires respect, sensitivity, and steady emotions. What emotions come to the surface as you work with a dead body?

*

STEPHEN BARON
Stephen is a 64-year-old funeral service
licensee in Grand Haven, Michigan

I think I speak for many of my colleagues that although we spend much of our time working with and around deceased individuals, as professionals we do not obsess over the body itself. While preparing the body, whatever that entails for that particular case, the body becomes the object of professional skill—the task at hand, so to speak. Also, just like any other healthy-minded person, funeral professionals do not operate in an emotional void. If anything, the opposite is true.

Many times, very well-meaning people will say to me something like, "I'm sure death doesn't even bother you. You are around it all the time, you must get used to it." Statements like this could not be further from the truth. When death strikes close to a funeral professional, it is just the same as it is for anyone else.

While working with the dead, I often find that my thoughts turn toward what is happening for survivors. The spouse, the children and all those lives that are suddenly upside down now have an emptiness and uncertainty that needs to be dealt with. When I approach my emotions from that angle, I remind myself that I have a very important and crucial job to do. I am also reminded of people in my profession that did their job well during times of loss in my own life.

*

CHASTIN BRINKLEY
Chastin is a 47-year-old funeral director, embalmer
and cremation specialist in Buckley, Washington

Only when I was in high school and walked through the funeral home at night did I ever feel a little scared. When young, it's very easy to let your mind wander and imagine terrible things. It is especially scary walking through the casket selection room with the lights off and twenty-two open caskets. Now, the darkness doesn't faze me and I have yet to see a ghost. In the HBO series Six Feet Under, when

David, the funeral director, embalmed or cosmetized someone, the same decedent would also be standing or sitting next to David carrying on a conversation with him. To me, that would be fascinating.

Caring for little babies and children can be sad. It's natural instinct to want to pick them up, hold them, and let them know everything will be okay. Working on babies is hard because their vessels are so tiny and fragile. I've worked with funeral directors who refused to go into the preparation room if a child was in there. They offered no explanation. I have never understood this, however I don't have children of my own. I have embalmed my grandmother, a close neighbor, several coworkers, their spouses, and the funeral home owner's family members. It was an honor to prepare them.

*

JENNI BRYANT
Jenni is a 41-year-old funeral director
and embalmer in Maryville, Tennessee

I am always aware that a body is someone's mother or father, brother or sister, son or daughter, loved one, or friend.

*

LAUREN BUDROW
Lauren is a 44-year-old funeral director
and funeral service educator

I struggle with the circumstances under which people have died. Once I began working in funeral service, I was unable to watch television shows or movies involving torture or murder. I grew intolerant to cruelty. I've seen bodies neglected, bruised and broken. I have seen people of all ages feel helpless to the point of ending their lives in various ways. I have seen infants autopsied to discover shaken baby syndrome, not sudden infant death syndrome. I've seen remnants of a drunk driver's carelessness. I've seen an elderly man who was beaten to death.

I'm inspired by the community support once a death occurs but disgusted by the lack of support when someone suffers prior to death. The body is proof of that lack of support, and is why we need to look at every dead body to try to understand why the event occurred (if) in an unnatural way. It says more about the living than the deceased.

*

SHARON GEE-MASCARELLO
Sharon is a 53-year-old funeral director and embalming instructor in the Mortuary Science Program at Wayne State University in Detroit

I tell my students, "Your hands are your expressions of humanity. You are the last ones to perform an act of kindness for this individual." I have repeated this to myself so many times that it has truly become part of my fabric. I am always honored to care for the dead. I consider it the highest privilege.

*

LOUISE GOHMANN
Louise is a 61-year-old mortuary school educator and funeral director in Jeffersonville, Indiana

Emotions when working with the dead can vary. I have felt overwhelming peace, and have said many times that working with dead bodies has reconfirmed my faith that when we die we go somewhere. I have picked up bodies from hospitals, nursing homes, and residences. Many times the facial expression is one of surprise and pleasure. I have never picked up anyone who looked frightened. I have felt sorrow when working with young people or children, and have prayed and sung in the prep room. I am very often struck by the irony of what we do. The week before Christmas, I watched a student doing her proficiency embalming, her "solo flight." As she was working away, I was struck by the absurdity of what we were doing while the radio was blaring Burl Ives singing "Have a Holly Jolly Christmas."

*

KAREN JELLY
Karen is a 44-year-old funeral director
and mortician in Havre, Montana

When working on a deceased individual, many emotions can surface. If I didn't know the person, it's often easier to take care of them. When I know them, however, I often grieve while caring for them. To me, it's always an honor to care for a deceased individual whether I knew them or not. My ability to close off my emotions while working on a person has increased over the years, but when I get home, they often flood to the surface. The most difficult part of working on a person is when they are very young or in a disfiguring accident. I've cared for babies, toddlers, school-aged children, and teenagers, and all of them cut me deeply. When a person is in a disfiguring accident, my goal is to restore them to how they looked in life, and sometimes I cannot. That is so difficult, because as a mother, I want their loved ones to see the person they loved looking peaceful.

*

CORIANN MARTIN
Coriann is a 42-year-old funeral director
and embalmer in Kenosha, Wisconsin

As an embalmer, I can't say that emotions enter the picture too much for me as I work with human remains. I find that staying focused on doing the best job of creating an image that the family can find peace with, is my ultimate goal. I want them to come in and say, "Wow, they haven't looked like that for so long." It's using my skills and expertise to do the best I can to have an open casket for the family. There are the occasions when I work on the young, the children, the babies, the ones who shouldn't be there. It doesn't mean I don't see the tragedy in that, but my job as a professional is to focus on the task at hand, which is to be respectful and allow the family to say goodbye and see their loved ones as they once were.

*

LACY ROBINSON
Lacy is a 38-year-old Director of Member Development for the
National Funeral Directors Association in Brookfield, Wisconsin

When working as a funeral director and embalmer, I always had a wide range of feelings when caring for a family's loved one. I always felt honored that this person's family entrusted our funeral home. I also had a lot of curiosity about the person, the life they lived, and the special relationships they had. There was also a strong desire to make sure the deceased's appearance was natural. It was important to me that a family's final moment with their loved one's physical body helped them emotionally on their journey of remembrance.

I've been fortunate to learn from the most talented licensed embalmers and restorative artists. One of those is Vernie Fountain, owner of Fountain National Academy in Springfield, Missouri. His favorite saying is, "Think it through." Vernie strongly encourages professional embalmers to maintain a sense of control and direction when caring for the deceased. Each person is unique and the circumstances in which they died can have an impact on their overall appearance. Bathing, disinfecting, embalming, cosmetizing and dressing all take time and a strong attention to detail.

When it comes to reconstructive surgery and restorative art, the best way to start is to "Think it through." When a family plans to view their loved one, it is so much more than walking into a room to see that person. Viewing provides the opportunity for families to acknowledge the reality of their loved one's death and transition into a life without that person. Professional embalmers contribute to that experience in a very positive way.

*

SHAWNA RODABAUGH
Shawna is a 37-year-old funeral director and
embalmer in Mount Pleasant, Michigan

After almost fifteen years in the industry, the one resounding emotion that comes up every time I work with someone's loved one is respect. I respect the life in front of me. I've even been known to have conversations with them while I work. It's comforting to me to explain what I'm doing to the deceased, and to just have conversations with them while I'm in the prep room. It seems a little unusual, but it keeps me in touch with the fact that the person in front of me is unique, and that there is a family waiting to see them. It helps me keep my humanity through the process.

*

STEVE TWEEDLE
Steve is a 42-year-old funeral
director in Ocala, Florida

I remember when I first started working at the funeral home, I was scared to death of the bodies. Since I mowed the lawn, I didn't have much of a reason to go into the building, so I was safe! On one occasion, I had to go in and get more trash bags. I walked by the room where they were set up for a visitation and it was a surreal moment for me. I was probably fourteen or fifteen. After I started working in the building, I was exposed to a whole different set of circumstances. I was asked to assist in getting them ready for viewing and services. I was told when I was ready I could go in and help. It took me a while to build up the courage to go in the preparation area. Looking back now, this was probably the turning point for me.

There was a funeral director working there who I didn't care for as a person. I was on his shift and had grown to resent the way he treated me. Let me be clear—he was good to the families he served, very good. He just didn't know how to be a good leader.

The first time I watched the preparation process, it changed the way I saw what the funeral home did, and the way I saw him. It was kind of like when you reach that age when you appreciate your parents again. As a child, they hung the moon. In your teenage years you think they're idiots. Then there's a point in your life when you realize how wrong you were when you were a teenager. That was what I experienced. I saw him treat that person with such honor and respect. I learned that this was someone's mother and that it was our privilege to be asked to prepare her for the viewing and service. That's when I decided that I wanted to do that. I was being called to serve right then and there. I'm so appreciative that my heart was open enough to hear and feel what was happening.

*

BRIAN VAN HECK
Brian is a 41-year-old funeral director in
the Lake Norman area of North Carolina

In my first six months working in the funeral home I was sent on a late evening transfer at a rural hospital. My travels took me on some very dark roads lined with cornfields, with very little traffic. While I thought nothing of this route and the surroundings on the way to the hospital with nothing on the cot or in the back of my vehicle, the drive back was a different story. Once away from the lights of the small town, with cornfields lining both sides of the dark, two lane road, my mind started playing tricks on me. Fear started to creep in: "What if he isn't dead? I've read about and seen movies with situations like this..." Totally irrational but that is what fear is. I found myself with a slightly increasing heart rate, but mainly an increasing speedometer needle. I made it back to the funeral home safely with the gentleman who was and, in fact, remained dead.

The fear that was present very early on has transformed into a deep sense of honor for being able to care for this life that was lived. Many times there is sadness as I have to watch the spouse of sixty or seventy years release his wife or her husband into the care of someone they barely know—me, their funeral director. While sadness is the most common emotion displayed by the family, anger is often present as well and I have had to learn how to handle that during the arrangement process and throughout the time serving that family. I have had to excuse myself from the office and a family feud that was happening directly before me, stating, "We cannot achieve what we need to right now until you can resolve the issue at hand." Most often, and sadly, the issue at hand is anger and greed over money or possessions.

*

KIMBERLY VARELA

Kimberly is a 41-year-old funeral director
and embalmer in Westland, Michigan

I sometimes feel very sympathetic when I receive someone who has obviously had a long battle with an illness. When the pain and effects of illness are etched on their face or on their body, you can't help but feel sympathy for their battle. I also feel a maternal emotion toward every decedent. I am their voice and their protector. I am taking care of someone's child, parent, spouse, and so on. That's huge. The level of care and time that goes into a proper arrangement builds the groundwork for a relationship and trust with the next of kin. But they have to believe that you will take care of their loved one. They may never see them after they are turned over to my care, or they may see them on several separate occasions depending on their choice of services. The deceased cannot defend their dignity, speak out at abuse or question your level of care for them. Everyone must be treated equally and shown a level of compassion, care and attention to their needs that they cannot speak openly.

*

DAN WELCH
Dan is a 30-year-old funeral director and
embalmer in Wichita, Kansas

There are two emotions I regularly feel when working on a dead body. The first being humility. I'm often humbled by the fact that a family—most often complete strangers—are fully and completely entrusting me with their loved one. Often times the interaction between a family and myself will last ten to fifteen minutes before I take their mom or their dad into my care. And to think that they are open and willing to that is a very humbling thing to think about.

Aside from humility, the second emotion I feel when working on a dead body is fascination. I'm fascinated with the intricacies of the human body. The purposeful design becomes so incredibly evident when having the opportunity to work on the human body. For the many years that I have been doing this, I am still engulfed in the uniqueness, yet distinct similarities, behind all human bodies. It is truly a fascinating thing.

*

Life is a great sunrise. I do not see why death
should not be an even greater one.

VLADIMIR NABOKOV

*

CHAPTER FOURTEEN

Taking care of Business

I want to work for a company that contributes to
and is part of the community. -ANITA RODDICK

The funeral industry is no different than any other business. The delicate handling of deceased loved ones requires a college education, using expensive equipment, and following strict codes. In addition, the demands of owning a business means paying staff who help meet the demands of round-the-clock customers. What is the hardest part about discussing costs and money with the bereaved family?

*

STEPHEN BARON
Stephen is a 64-year-old funeral service
licensee in Grand Haven, Michigan

I have always found that the absolute hardest part of the financial discussion is making sure the responsible party has a clear understanding of all the transactions. Experience has shown me that most people are prepared for the fact that a funeral director's services, as with any professional service, come with charges. The area of concern for me comes with the client's ability to understand those charges and the services selected. After all, the circumstances surrounding this type of purchase are never convenient, and often emotions can cloud otherwise good, sound judgment and thereby make matters hard to understand.

Several years ago, the Federal Trade Commission (FTC) began to require funeral homes to make full disclosure of prices and explanation of services upfront in the arrangement conference. By doing so, they did both the consumer and funeral directors a big favor. Perhaps someday the FTC will require the same of the legal and medical professions. I am always more at ease when a family realizes that their ability to take all the information in during the arrangement's conference may be compromised, and as a result they engage an advocate. The result is that we are all better served.

*

CHASTIN BRINKLEY
Chastin is a 47-year-old funeral director, embalmer
and cremation specialist in Buckley, Washington

Discussing costs and money has never been hard for me because I view our service like any other business transaction. For example, we all need to eat but you cannot go into a restaurant, order a meal and expect not to pay for it. Similarly, folks should expect to pay for death care. What bothers me is when an elderly person dies and their spouse or other family members ask us who is going to pay for our services. Most adults have their whole lives to plan and save for their death expenses. To that end, most North American funeral homes allow monthly payments into an insurance or trust account.

After the first year of our marriage, my wife and I took out life insurance on ourselves as well as long-term care insurance because we knew we would not have any children to pay our funeral costs. We also both felt it was not the responsibility of the taxpayers to pay for our disposition. However, I am fortunate to work with a funeral home that goes above and beyond to help families have a service if they are truly destitute.

Every once in a while a family will experience "sticker shock" and make a comment such as, "We are in the wrong business." I don't get upset because most people do not know what costs are involved to run a business. Usually after I explain these costs, our clients understand. I have even asked customers what they think would be a fair cost for the type of work we do, working around the clock including holidays. Their response, "Not enough!"

*

JENNI BRYANT
Jenni is a 41-year-old funeral director
and embalmer in Maryville, Tennessee

Money is always a touchy subject. Some families realize that payment is due at the time of service and come in with checkbook in hand and will not leave the arrangement conference without paying in full. Those people are becoming few and far between. I think it's hard for some people to understand that funeral homes are for-profit businesses. So in order for us to keep the lights on, I have to collect money. We have a payment policy in place, with several options for families. We try to never turn a family away that can't afford to pay; we are, after all, here to help them!

*

LAUREN BUDROW
Lauren is a 44-year-old funeral director
and funeral service educator

The hardest part about discussing costs and money with a family is maintaining the line between being compassionate and yet still being an employee of a business. People have tried to haggle over price with me. I told a man his mother's funeral would cost $5,500 and he asked if I would take $5,000 instead. I thought he was joking at first. He had the money, he just didn't want to spend it on his mother's funeral. It was difficult for me not to display my disbelief in this man's conduct when we were discussing services for his dead mother.

Another difficult aspect of discussing money with a family is when they refuse to alter their merchandise and service choices to bring the costs to an affordable level for themselves. The funeral director gets blamed for the bottom line expense, but that expense oftentimes is because the family refuses to spend less on other things, which isn't an issue so long as they can afford them. Funeral homes are not extending credit or taking payment plans as they have been willing to do in the past, so funeral directors are asking for payment to be in full before services are rendered. Once a funeral service is over, there's no repossessing the casket, vault, flowers or honorariums so we are asking for a large commitment in a short period of time. The combination of the short time frame with the amount of money creates a tension between the funeral director and the family.

*

JASON RYAN ENGLER
Jason is a 36-year-old funeral director, certified celebrant,
and cremation historian in Rogers, Arkansas

I am a firm believer of the importance of the business side of our profession. When you have a desire to serve people, it is indeed a gift to be able to care for them. However, just as many sides of our lives require a financial commitment on behalf of those being served, funeral and memorial experiences cannot happen without cost. Therefore, I have no qualms about bringing up financial discussions with a family. I am confident that what I do is of value and importance to the family, and am committed to making their investment memorable and important.

*

SHARON GEE-MASCARELLO
Sharon is a 53-year-old funeral director and embalming instructor
in the Mortuary Science Program at Wayne State University in Detroit

Earlier I called the funeral "life's final event." I emphasize that like a wedding, baptism, graduation or retirement, we plan for and celebrate life's events. Some events require lengthy planning and great cost. The funeral too, requires planning and cost. However, we plan immediately when the death occurs, the time of ceremony is quite

223

short, and the cost is variable and entirely up to the family. This shifts the power to the arranging family. I further explain that I am simply acting as a conduit, to perform the necessary steps and hold it all together, like a director in a play. I believe I put people at ease when I tell them that I work for them.

*

LOUISE GOHMANN
Louise is a 61-year-old mortuary school educator
and funeral director in Jeffersonville, Indiana

I don't find it too difficult discussing costs and money with families. Most people understand that ours is a business just like any other business, and there are costs involved. Perhaps it's because I spent so many years selling cemetery and preneed funerals that I am comfortable as a whole in broaching the subject of cost and payment.

With the rise in cremation, many people have become savvy shoppers. It is not uncommon to find families who choose a funeral home based on the cost of goods and services. The only time it becomes difficult is when a family asks if they can make payments on Grandma's funeral. I have never worked in a funeral home that allowed payments after a death, but I have talked with many small town funeral directors who do. Sometimes it works out, but very often it doesn't. The old saying, "Out of sight, out of mind," is very true in the funeral business!

*

KAREN JELLY
Karen is a 44-year-old funeral director
and mortician in Havre, Montana

The hardest part of discussing costs and money with the family is when the family is not prepared for the costs. Many people do not even have life insurance, and this leaves those they love in a horrible financial bind. When speaking with the families about these costs, I use our general price list, and speak with them matter-of-factly. I explain the costs to the best of my ability, and offer them choices. For instance, some families would like a more expensive casket because they like how it looks better than the less expensive ones, but they cannot afford it. I encourage them to speak with the florist about ways to dress it up with the casket spray so they are able to save the several hundred dollars that they need for other expenses.

I have been accused a few times over the years of trying to profit from death. Usually, my response is that I would never do that but I do understand that this is difficult. I also explain that costs continue to rise, and that we try to keep them down as much as we can for families.

Fortunately, our funeral home has been located in this town for 110 years, and we are fairly trusted. Most people know we truly care about the families, and I don't run into this attitude often. I also know that this attitude can come from the grief people are feeling, and they need to get it out. Sometimes, I am the recipient of that. I don't take it personally.

*

CORIANN MARTIN
Coriann is a 42-year-old funeral director
and embalmer in Kenosha, Wisconsin

When it comes time to discuss finances with families who've just suffered a loss, I struggle with them misunderstanding my motives. I try to always explain that, by nature, I'm a frugal person so I let them know that I will suggest ways to save money whenever possible. I think when you explain that you understand the financial hardship that an unexpected or sudden death can put a family under, especially when the next of kin are younger or unprepared, they feel more at ease discussing budgets and making financial decisions.

If I ever encounter accusations of being unethical or trying to take advantage of people, I try to explain that the financial decisions they make are personal and my job is to help inform them of all their choices. Ultimately, in the end, they are responsible and need to feel comfortable with the choices they make and commit to paying for.

*

LACY ROBINSON
Lacy is a 38-year-old Director of Member Development for the
National Funeral Directors Association in Brookfield, Wisconsin

Discussing with families their financial obligation can sometimes be a very difficult conversation. Many families who are making funeral plans are experiencing an unexpected death. Mentally and emotionally, family members are not prepared. On top of that, they may not be financially prepared for funeral expenses. The Federal

Reserve recently reported, "Nearly half of US families would find it difficult to deal with an unexpected $400 expense." Funeral directors take this all into consideration when discussing with families their financial obligation.

For families concerned about the financial burden of funeral expenses, funeral directors will create an open dialogue about their budget, explain in detail the funeral home's payment policy and the different choices the family has to honor their loved one's life. It's important that every family served understands the value of the services and merchandise they select. Funeral directors will ensure families understand the value by giving a thorough explanation of every charge. Families are in complete control of how much or how little money they want to spend. Funeral directors want families to leave the arrangement conference feeling confident with the decisions and selections they made for remembering their loved one's life.

*

SHAWNA RODABAUGH
Shawna is a 37-year-old funeral director and
embalmer in Mount Pleasant, Michigan

This is my least favorite part of being a funeral director. I have always had an issue discussing costs with a family, especially if I know that what they want is beyond the means that they have. If a family tells me what their budget is, and then tells me about products and services that are beyond that budget, it is heartbreaking to tell them that, financially, those products are out of reach. I've always tried to offer alternatives rather than just giving prices, so families can feel good about their selections before leaving the funeral home. I never want to have a family leave my home thinking that they are getting a lesser funeral service than they want.

*

STEVE TWEEDLE
Steve is a 42-year-old funeral
director in Ocala, Florida

Discussing money, initially, was hard for me. I was brought up in this business the old school way. I have seen the funeral home take collard greens for payment. I have seen the funeral home get painted because the family couldn't pay the funeral bill, so they painted the building for us. I realized though that this doesn't keep the lights on, and on a personal level I have bills too. So I had to rationalize it when the ownership came to us and said that we needed to start asking for payment. What I learned very quickly is that people know they have to pay. We just never asked. When we started asking, people were prepared. We just thought they weren't.

For people who didn't understand that or couldn't pay, we always worked with them. We would always try to get them to reduce the services down to what they needed, not what they wanted. If a family was willing to reduce services down to basics, we would work with them as far as payment. What I realized was that giving people what they wanted and telling them, "Just pay when you can," wasn't beneficial to them. It saddled them with a huge bill and more than likely would result in us sending them to collections. At the end of the day, they would be resentful of us and us of them. Who was that serving?

One thing I have never been accused of is trying to profit from death. I have been accused of having prices that are too high. As a professional, you have to be ready to defend what you do. The one thing funeral directors universally failed at was explaining to people what they were paying for. Historically we have always said to people, "We'll take care of it," as we tried to relieve them of some of the stress and burdens of what they were going through. Instead of explaining to them everything we do, we always said, "Don't worry about it, we'll take care of it." We never said, "Yes we can take care of it and this is how."

Most people don't realize the amount of man hours it takes, from taking the first call, to dispatching the removal personnel, to the preparation staff preparing the body, to the funeral director meeting the family, to the funeral director making the needed phone calls, coordinating with the minister, the musicians, and the cemeteries. The administrative staff getting the needed signatures for death certificates, the permits, and the printed material. Then there's the coordinating of the staff and vehicles, washing the vehicles, making sure the building is ready for the funeral. All of this before the actual funeral itself. I always tell people what we can do and how we do it. I never say to them, "Don't worry about it, we'll take care of it." It devalues me as a professional.

*

BRIAN VAN HECK
Brian is a 41-year-old funeral director in
the Lake Norman area of North Carolina

I became a funeral director because I wanted to help families at a time of great need. Therefore, getting comfortable discussing charges and reviewing the financial contracts with the bereaved took some time. Today I believe so strongly in what I do and the exceptionally high level of service that my team and I provide, that I do not feel uncomfortable talking about the charges for our services. I have been blessed to work for funeral homes where the families expect to pay and do pay for the service that we provide, which make the financial conversations and business aspect of our work a little easier.

One shift that has grown significantly over the past ten years or so is price shopping either via phone or walking into the funeral home to obtain pricing. The price shoppers, especially phone shoppers, provide more challenges and push back on our charges. The difficulty is that they have likely not had any experience with us, have not seen our facility and have not met us, so they have no idea what we can and do provide. They are strictly motivated by price, and to me that is not only challenging but also sad.

*

DAN WELCH
Dan is a 30-year-old funeral director and
embalmer in Wichita, Kansas

Although discussing costs and money with families can be

difficult, I have been blessed to have had the opportunity to work for a firm that will work with any family regardless of their financial situation. The challenge with this, however, comes when a family who truly has no money still wants to have a lavish funeral. The most difficult part then becomes educating the family on the realistic expectations they should have, given their financial situation.

Overall, I have had very little issue with families not paying their bills. I have found if you give a family options within their price range, they will be satisfied and ultimately be a repeat customer for generations to come.

*

If a funeral director helps plan, coordinate
and execute a meaningful funeral,
survivors will feel so much better.

CHASTIN BRINKLEY

*

CHAPTER FIFTEEN

Dealing with Grief

The purpose of human life is to serve, and to show compassion and the will to help others. –ALBERT SCHWEITZER

Although caregivers at heart, funeral directors have to become accustomed to working with death on a daily basis. Further, it takes a unique person to deal with the grief of others as part of their everyday duties. In response, do you feel your career in the funeral industry has made you more compassionate or more desensitized to death?

*

STEPHEN BARON
Stephen is a 64-year-old funeral service
licensee in Grand Haven, Michigan

Without question, my career in funeral service has broadened my capacity for compassion. We all come with a different set of gifts and talents. Hopefully those entering any and all careers covered under the category of caregiving, have at least a hint of compassion for their fellow human beings and an appreciation for the fact that each one of us carry a burden of some sort much of the time. I believe that the seed for compassion is planted in all of us. Only by exercising our care for others and accepting caring gestures offered to us, can our understanding and empathetic attitudes broaden. A career in funeral service without the ability to be compassionate, becomes nothing more than a monetary business.

*

CHASTIN BRINKLEY
Chastin is a 47-year-old funeral director, embalmer
and cremation specialist in Buckley, Washington

I think I am the same. There are some deaths when the family is relieved the person died because the person was in so much pain. Then there are the deaths that are tragic, sad, or both, usually the young. These are the deaths that pull at your heartstrings. Hollywood has done a great job of depicting trauma and carnage on the big screen. If you have seen the movie *Rambo*, you will not have to wonder what kind of damage a bullet can do to the human body. Arguments have been made about how violent movies and video games could make you more prone to violence. I believe it just shows you what to expect. Even though Hollywood can glamorize or villainize death, they cannot change your feelings or emotions when you experience death. Because feelings and emotions are what they are, they are unique to the person experiencing them.

*

JENNI BRYANT
Jenni is a 41-year-old funeral director
and embalmer in Maryville, Tennessee

I guess it depends on the day! Most days I feel a little more desensitized to the death than other days. I think it is my way of coping with being surrounded by death every single day.

*

LAUREN BUDROW
Lauren is a 44-year-old funeral director
and funeral service educator

For me, I feel more compassionate and protective of the dead now that I have worked with them and their families. I was asked if I live my life differently since joining funeral service, and I truly believe that I do. I am more sympathetic to the people around me because I wonder if their rude or uncharacteristic behavior is the result of a recent loss. I look at my own actions more critically now because I want people to think better, not worse, of me if this is the last time we meet.

I cringe at the funeral director and service spoofs on television and in the movies. I can take a joke about my profession, but I don't like being the punchline for every joke about death care, and I really do not appreciate the public's assumption that all funeral directors are scoundrels. Unfortunately, Hollywood perpetuates that ridiculous notion.

*

JASON RYAN ENGLER
Jason is a 36-year-old funeral director, certified celebrant,
and cremation historian in Rogers, Arkansas

On a level of the general public, being the unmovable person who remains strong for a family may seem like a desensitized feeling toward death. This isn't entirely accurate. Perhaps it is more that the fear of death has subsided than that the sensitivity toward death has retreated. Having less fear of death, and the commitment we have to allow for the memory of the dead to remain in our lives, takes away the sensitivity of death and allows us to be much more compassionate.

*

SHARON GEE-MASCARELLO
Sharon is a 53-year-old funeral director and embalming instructor
in the Mortuary Science Program at Wayne State University in Detroit

It is both blessing and curse to live life as a funeral director. I wear compassion on my sleeve most all the time, except when I fail to react, outside of the funeral setting, to the news of someone's passing. Because I hear it so regularly, I take the news in stride and can forget to respond with sadness or surprise. My reaction is to start working instead.

*

LOUISE GOHMANN
Louise is a 61-year-old mortuary school educator
and funeral director in Jeffersonville, Indiana

Has my career made me more compassionate? Yes. I love the feeling I get when I am able to help a family in some way. Sometimes the smallest act can have the greatest impact on them and on me. Has it made me more desensitized to death? Yes. It seems almost comical to discuss lunch or the results of last night's ballgame while dressing or cosmetizing a body, or arranging flowers in a visitation parlor, but life goes on, as it should.

*

KAREN JELLY
Karen is a 44-year-old funeral director
and mortician in Havre, Montana

I believe my career has made me more compassionate toward death. I experience it almost daily, and I see its emotionally devastating results. I believe, however, that the public has become so desensitized toward death, due in large part to the television shows and movies that depict death. The young people, especially, see someone die in a movie or television show, and then a few weeks or months later, that person is in another movie or show. This skews their view of what death really is and how permanent it is.

*

CORIANN MARTIN
Coriann is a 42-year-old funeral director
and embalmer in Kenosha, Wisconsin

Being in the funeral service industry definitely makes you a more compassionate person but I think people misunderstand comfort for becoming desensitized. As a funeral director with stage four cancer, I have found that my job allows me to be more comfortable discussing the reality of life and death. These topics aren't so easy for non-funeral service professionals to understand, let alone hearing someone's wishes. Death is a natural part of life but it isn't natural to talk about. It's never easy to talk about death but in talking about our lives and what you want to be remembered for, here lies the way you can celebrate a life.

Our society wants to sweep death under the rug and just get through the funeral. When they meet with a funeral director and see our comfort level discussing end-of-life issues, we get misunderstood for being cold or calloused. When a family has to endure the planning stage of a funeral, the public gets to see the business side of a funeral. I compare this to watching a live play from backstage. When you see the inner workings of something you only usually see from the sidelines, you see it in a different light.

*

LACY ROBINSON
Lacy is a 38-year-old Director of Member Development for the
National Funeral Directors Association in Brookfield, Wisconsin

With the growth of social media I have seen an interesting shift in how people talk about death and show compassion to others who are experiencing grief. When there's a tragic event, people do unite as a country, as a state, in big cities and small towns. Stories of people who have died, as well as stories of people who are facing death in the very near future, become widely publicized. It's these stories that prompt people to share their thoughts and condolences. It always motivates people to help in some way. I truly believe people have become more compassionate, but also more comfortable, with sharing their personal stories related to death, as well as reaching out to others who are experiencing grief.

Hollywood's depiction of death through movies and television is always up for debate. The far more interesting role Hollywood plays in how the public views death is when a celebrity or noteworthy person dies. Muhammad Ali's death is a great example of someone who took an active role in planning an amazing remembrance event ten years prior to death. He planned every detail of his service and wanted to include the world. As a funeral director, I appreciate Muhammad Ali's desire to put powerful funeral traditions and rituals on full display for the world to see. It sends a very positive message about the importance of honoring and remembering people's lives.

*

SHAWNA RODABAUGH
Shawna is a 37-year-old funeral director and
embalmer in Mount Pleasant, Michigan

I definitely feel that it has made me more compassionate to be in funeral service. I have been on both sides of the arrangement desk, and I will admit that there are days when I can become desensitized to a point, but one look at a family brings me right back to center. It is important for me as a human being to never forget why I'm in the position that I'm in, and that is to provide comfort and a place for healthy grief for a family going through the roughest time in their lives. If I ever forget that, I will find another profession.

*

STEVE TWEEDLE
Steve is a 42-year-old funeral
director in Ocala, Florida

I was thinking about this the other day. I'm not afraid of dying. I think that is because of what I do. I would think most people are. They aren't faced with it every day, and it's something they shy away from dealing with. For me it's a fear of my kids not having me there; I'm not afraid, I'm afraid of what they would go through. I always find it ironic when nurses say, "I could never do what you do!" For me it's the opposite. I couldn't deal with the suffering. I deal with families and I know that, although they are starting to work through some hard days, life goes on.

*

BRIAN VAN HECK
Brian is a 41-year-old funeral director in
the Lake Norman area of North Carolina

Nearly two decades working in and around funeral homes has allowed me to have a comfort with death that the general population doesn't possess, but I don't feel it has desensitized me to death. For me, good self-care helps me stay grounded and avoid burnout. When the death of a young child or watching an elderly man saying goodbye to his sweetheart doesn't evoke sadness in me, I need to take a good look and identify what is going on. Poor self-care? Burnout? Desensitized? Whatever the answer, I need to make the necessary adjustments so I can be the best version of myself in order to be the best funeral director for the families who call upon me to care for their loved one.

CHAPTER SIXTEEN

Accepting Our Path

Life is made up not of great sacrifices or duties, but of little things in which smiles and kindness, and small obligations given habitually, are what preserve the heart and secure comfort. -HUMPHRY DAVY

Some funeral directors are born into the family business. Others are drawn by a desire to help the bereaved. One thing is certain: working in the funeral industry is a lifelong commitment. If you could go back and choose a different career, would you choose something different?

*

STEPHEN BARON
Stephen is a 64-year-old funeral service
licensee in Grand Haven, Michigan

I would not be truthful if I said I've never entertained the idea of other careers. I think that by doing so, you also take inventory of your chosen profession. While in college, I seriously looked at a career in pharmacy. In more recent times I think I may have had some talent in the area of human resources. In all truthfulness, most of the time I'm satisfied with my choice of serving in the funeral profession.

*

CHASTIN BRINKLEY
Chastin is a 47-year-old funeral director, embalmer
and cremation specialist in Buckley, Washington

If I had gone into the Marine Corps after high school, I would have been retired by now and probably would have gravitated toward a second career in funeral service because of my high school buddy. Knowing what I know now, I am glad that I was lucky enough to serve my apprenticeship when I did because times have changed along with attitudes. The attitudes that I speak of refer to the work ethic you must have. This work ethic was instilled in me early in my career. That is you didn't go home until the work was done. The millennials entering the workforce want to hit the door at five o'clock, even when there are a good four hours of work left in the preparation room. When speaking at our local high school, I don't discourage a career in funeral service, but I do warn of long hours and sometimes grueling schedules.

*

JENNI BRYANT
Jenni is a 41-year-old funeral director
and embalmer in Maryville, Tennessee

I would not choose a different career. I love the funeral business. I like the good, the bad, and the ugly. I like being able to help people when they need it most. Every year I participate in career day at the local high school and encourage kids to look into the funeral industry. If you enjoy helping others, are interested in biological science, and want to make a positive contribution to your community, then being a funeral director might be a profession to consider.

*

LAUREN BUDROW
Lauren is a 44-year-old funeral director
and funeral service educator

I love funeral service even though I've modified my role within the profession to be in the classroom as a funeral service educator instead of being in a funeral home. I think funeral service is an amazing career path. It brought forth the compassionate side within me so I could help people when they were hurting. It exposed me to the complexity of compassion juxtaposed with business practicality, and I gained a better appreciation for how to handle a variety of emotional states during such a difficult time. I learned how to adapt and be flexible without letting a family know anything was going wrong. I was given access to private moments and wonderful stories of lives I wished I had known or wanted to emulate in the future.

I began to understand grief within myself during loss. I learned more about society by studying its response to death. No other career that I know of can do that. We work with the here and the after, and funeral service is the gateway to acceptance and healing between the two.

*

JASON RYAN ENGLER
Jason is a 36-year-old funeral director, certified celebrant,
and cremation historian in Rogers, Arkansas

Absolutely not. Even after blood, sweat and tears, I would do it all over again!

*

SHARON GEE-MASCARELLO
Sharon is a 53-year-old funeral director and embalming instructor
in the Mortuary Science Program at Wayne State University in Detroit

Yes and no. My life is enriched by my vocational choice. I wouldn't be who I am without funeral service. Yet, there are days when I fantasize what my life would hold as the proprietor of a string of cottage and kayak rentals. I desire to be in the woods and on the water simultaneously. A girl can dream.

*

LOUISE GOHMANN
Louise is a 61-year-old mortuary school educator
and funeral director in Jeffersonville, Indiana

If I could go back and choose another career, I don't think I would choose something different. Everything in my life, including my career choices, has brought be to where I am today. I love being a funeral director, and I love being a teacher, training the funeral directors of the future. I cannot see myself doing anything different for the rest of my working life.

*

KAREN JELLY
Karen is a 44-year-old funeral director
and mortician in Havre, Montana

If I could go back and choose a different career, I would do it all again. I truly love what I do, even when I'm sleep deprived and haggard. I would, however, encourage those in the younger generation who are interested in this type of work, to work in a funeral home before attending school. The experience, whether in an office, removing people from the hospital, nursing home, or residence, or assisting at services, is invaluable, and will help them decide if this life is really the right choice for them. A funeral director's life, at least in a smaller town, really does revolve around work. On call, visitations, Saturday services... they all take time from our personal lives, and it can be very, very hard to maintain the right attitude toward the grieving family.

*

CORIANN MARTIN
Coriann is a 42-year-old funeral director
and embalmer in Kenosha, Wisconsin

The only other career path I've ever considered was being a child psychologist. I think I've always wanted to help people through difficult times but trying to imagine myself as anything other than a funeral director just wouldn't make sense. I love what I do and any chance I get to counsel a student or have them job shadow for the day gives me a chance to show the younger generation what doors funeral service can open for them.

*

SHAWNA RODABAUGH
Shawna is a 37-year-old funeral director and
embalmer in Mount Pleasant, Michigan

I don't regret my decision to become a funeral director in the least bit. Although I no longer work in a traditional funeral environment, I don't think my life would be complete without doing what I truly feel I was called to do.

When young men and women come to me, interested in looking into this career, I encourage them to follow their calling. This is not an industry you can be in unless you really feel like this is something you were meant to do. I counsel them to explore their hearts, and discover why they want to pursue the field before considering it. It is a difficult field, and one that requires a love of the work.

*

STEVE TWEEDLE
Steve is a 42-year-old funeral
director in Ocala, Florida

Quite simply no. I wouldn't encourage people to get into this business. It's hard, stressful, full of long hours, you spend more time with other families than you do your own. I always tell people that you don't pick this job, this job picks you. I recently hired a young man who thought he wanted to be a funeral director. He had no intentions of being one, and when he came in I basically did all I could do to discourage him from working for us. He kept coming back. I hired him the third time he came back. I asked him why he kept coming back. He didn't know. He said he just had to be here. The job picked him. I told that story to someone the other day and they said it was the hand of God guiding him.

*

BRIAN VAN HECK
Brian is a 41-year-old funeral director in
the Lake Norman area of North Carolina

Absolutely not. The journey has been amazing and I welcome and look forward with eager anticipation to what God has in store.

*

DAN WELCH
Dan is a 30-year-old funeral director and
embalmer in Wichita, Kansas

If I could go back and choose a different career, I honestly do not think I would. I absolutely LOVE being a funeral director and embalmer, and I truly feel that it is my life's calling. What I would change would be the path that I took in order to become a funeral director. Ultimately I know that my pastoral schooling and training is a huge reason I am as successful as I am in this business. However, if I had to do it all over again, I feel as though I would pursue some more education on grief psychology or perhaps family studies. I feel that this type of education would certainly aid in better serving families.

*

We make a living by what we get;
we make a life by what we give

WINSTON CHURCHILL

*

CHAPTER SEVENTEEN

Designing Our Own Funeral

I didn't attend the funeral, but I sent a nice letter
saying I approved of it. -MARK TWAIN

Generational trends aside, today's funeral options are limited only by imagination. Interactive headstones, water cremations, memorial reefs, and participatory funerals that allow family to care for the body are but a few of the trends to consider. With so many choices available, what kind of funeral do you want for yourself, and why?

*

STEPHEN BARON
Stephen is a 64-year-old funeral service
licensee in Grand Haven, Michigan

"Dead people don't care," a quote from poet, author and fellow Michigan funeral director Thomas Lynch. This phrase often comes to mind when people start to expound on what it is they want their own funerals to include or not include. Whether we see any truth in his words or not, when pondered, a lot of us can't help but give this question some very serious thought. We all want to give those close to us some help in identifying our preferences. Mr. Lynch readily tells his audiences of the answer that he and his siblings were given by their funeral director father when they asked the question of him. "You will know what to do," was his answer.

I, like Ed Lynch, trust that my spouse and children will know what to do when that time comes. That being said, I will take this opportunity to remind them once more of a couple of the details. First off let me state an observation I have made about funeral wishes, that I consider to be more often the case than not. It is part of our humanness to either leave our loved ones with no direction or to give them far too many instructions. I consider the latter the more dangerous of the two and here is why. We need to recognize that there is truth in the oft quoted phrase, "Funerals are for the living." While much of what we do surrounding death and funerals is done to honor and pay tribute to the deceased, if all this does not help to get our survivors back on the track of a productive life and return them to some normalcy afterward, then it is just so much hocus pocus.

That is why it is so important for all of us to let our survivors have the major stake in the planning of our funerals. They are in grief, not us; we are dead and we do not care. I should hope that those I leave behind will look at my life as a life well lived and honor me with the sentiment, ceremony and liturgy that they feel is deserving of my interaction and my relationship with my God and all of His creation during my brief earthly stay. Other than that, the only instructions and desires I would voice would be the following. A Christian service held at my place of worship if at all possible. Make sure, as I have said, that your individual needs are met, give proper thanks to God for our relationships, do not hesitate to seek the help of each other and others that you need to move beyond that day, and go into the world giving honor and respect to all God's children.

*

CHASTIN BRINKLEY
Chastin is a 47-year-old funeral director, embalmer
and cremation specialist in Buckley, Washington

When I was in mortuary school, our class was assigned to plan our own funeral service. I am pretty sure everyone had a similar funeral other than the casket selected. I still have a copy of my paper in storage. Funerals back then were not personalized as they are today. There were no tribute videos or picture collages. Even the type of music was limited. Only the black community stood up at funerals and shared remembrances. Their service folders read, "Remarks...two minutes please," and the preacher would start on the front row. Wow! Everyone got to speak!

When my time does come, I would like my service to be at the funeral home. It would be great if all the ministers I worked with and a few families who I helped throughout the years would come and participate in my funeral. I would have a double grave so I could have a huge grave marker in the shape of Texas that would span the width of both graves. The marker would be so unique, our local marker company would win the national design competition.

251

In reality, when my wife and I retire, we will probably move to Arizona. I will outlive what family I have left. So, I envision a local minister will come to the nursing home to recite some scripture and say a prayer in the dining hall. The nurses and aides will all testify that I was their favorite resident. Then for lunch they will serve my favorite meal: hot dogs. And for those who are allowed sugar: a fun size Snickers Bar.

*

JENNI BRYANT
Jenni is a 41-year-old funeral director
and embalmer in Maryville, Tennessee

I do not want to be cremated. I believe in the art of embalming, the viewing of the body, and the celebration of a life lived. Not for me, but for those left when I'm gone. I want my family to be surrounded by people who can tell them wonderful stories about me, bring them all kinds of yummy food, and be an ear to listen. And in the end I want to be buried in a cemetery with a marker and a vase for flowers, somewhere that people can go to feel close to me if they want.

*

JASON RYAN ENGLER
Jason is a 36-year-old funeral director, certified celebrant,
and cremation historian in Rogers, Arkansas

I have very intense funeral instructions in place for my service of remembrance. I have a celebrant service planned with lots of music and stories, hopefully making it a highly personal remembrance for my family and friends. Following the service and reception, I will be cremated and my cremated remains inurned and placed in one of six historic columbaria across the country. I won't disclose the specific location until the publication of my obituary.

*

SHARON GEE-MASCARELLO
Sharon is a 53-year-old funeral director and embalming instructor
in the Mortuary Science Program at Wayne State University in Detroit

The funeral I wish for myself is authentic testimony to the love of my profession. I want to be embalmed with an open casket visitation in the lecture hall of the mortuary school. Family, friends and colleagues will mingle, sip flutes of champagne, and enjoy lovely eats. Oh, and harp music played by Mayim Bialik, television's Amy Farrah Fowler of The Big Bang Theory. More strolling musicians à la Jazz Funeral throughout the halls and staircases with a stopover in the embalming lab. And please bury me with my aneurysm hook.

*

LOUISE GOHMANN
Louise is a 61-year-old mortuary school educator
and funeral director in Jeffersonville, Indiana

Like most funeral directors I know, I have my own service all planned out. I have chosen the music, readings, a verse for my memorial cards, even the photo for a memorial portrait. I love Broadway show tunes, so it is my requested music for visitation. I plan on being cremated, but want a traditional visitation with the body, so people can see the quality of our work! My funeral will be at the funeral home because even though I am an Episcopalian, I want secular music at my service, therefore, it cannot be held at church. I would like a bagpiper to play "Skye Boat Song" at the end of the service. However, I would like my priest to have an Episcopalian committal service when my cremains are entombed next to my mother. I would like my service to be as early as possible in the morning just to annoy the heck out of my family; dawn would be ideal. I have always been an early riser, it drives my family crazy! Follow with a fellowship brunch, where they can complain at having to get up so early. Finally, I would like a spoonful of my cremains to be taken to my favorite beach. A small part of my soul has always found peace at the ocean.

*

KAREN JELLY
Karen is a 44-year-old funeral director
and mortician in Havre, Montana

I will have a traditional service with burial to follow. I was raised in a family who buries. I firmly believe that having a visitation and a service with the deceased loved one present really helps to begin the grieving process. Not seeing that person often leaves room for those in denial to say, "She didn't die. She's just not home right now. I'll see her soon." Once reality sets in later, I believe these people have a harder time accepting the death.

Many people change what they want, but I've always wanted this, and will probably always want this. I have a file of what I want, from the casket, to the songs, to the minister, and the poem for my service folder. I'm nothing if not prepared ... and a bit of a control freak.

*

CORIANN MARTIN
Coriann is a 42-year-old funeral director
and embalmer in Kenosha, Wisconsin

I still believe in tradition but what I've learned through my career is to celebrate! As I'm faced with my own mortality and am currently planning my own funeral, I find that I struggle with planning a funeral that I'd love to attend and one that will help those I leave behind. Again, as a funeral director, my comfort level discussing my death doesn't always balance out with my family's ability to hear it. I truly believe funerals are for the living, and people who come to your funeral already know you. I want a funeral that reminds people about the forgotten parts of me or the parts that not everyone knows. I want to end on a happy note. I want laughter and most of all, I want a room full of smiles.

*

LACY ROBINSON
Lacy is a 38-year-old Director of Member Development for the
National Funeral Directors Association in Brookfield, Wisconsin

I've spent a considerable amount of time thinking about and designing my end-of-life ceremony. I believe wholeheartedly in the purpose that funeral rituals serve in helping those who are grieving. For that reason I want to have a full traditional funeral service that demonstrates for family and friends that a visitation, funeral service, and committal ceremony followed by a reception are important mourning activities. I want guests to laugh, cry, share stories, be entertained by the music that I loved and savor all the foods I enjoyed throughout my life. I've had my funeral planned and final resting place selected for decades. (I've even taken friends to the cemetery to show off my final resting place). Over the years I've changed details and added new ideas to better reflect my personality, but for the most part the plan to have traditional funeral events have stayed consistent.

I don't want to give away too many details of my funeral service because the element of surprise and delight is an important part of the entire experience for guests. My family and friends can expect to hear Elvis, Lawrence Welk and of course Tina Turner. I have pictures from all years of my life in cue ready for the video tribute. I have not left out any part of my life or those who have impacted my life in some way. It would be nice to have my brother, who is a professional emcee facilitate the service with the help of several friends sharing stories. I want the symbolism of funeral service to be front and center. My body will be present since I am the guest of honor. I do plan on being embalmed because I truly believe it's an art performed by very talented and caring individuals. I would like to have different vignettes displaying my most meaningful belongings. This includes my collection of Lawrence Welk memorabilia and my aluminum Christmas trees with vintage ornaments. Everyone in attendance will receive a heartfelt keepsake (that's a tasteful way of saying party favor).

There will be a very slow procession to the cemetery because I believe it's important for everyone who loved the deceased to help accompany that person to their final resting place. I want passersby on the road to see my funeral procession to the cemetery and think about life and death on a much deeper level. I have planned an after ceremony reception showcasing all my favorite Kentucky foods. It's going to be a good time and I hope a lot of people will come and participate. I want people who knew me to be totally immersed in my funeral events and not shy away from attending any part of it. I'm planning this for those I love.

*

SHAWNA RODABAUGH
Shawna is a 37-year-old funeral director and
embalmer in Mount Pleasant, Michigan

I truly believe that funerals are for the living, not for the dead. Because of this, I have refrained from instructing my family about funeral services for myself. As far as I'm concerned, I want them to do what they feel comfortable with, without imposing my expectations onto them. I have money set aside for whatever they feel will be meaningful, but otherwise I want to leave the decision up to them.

*

STEVE TWEEDLE
Steve is a 42-year-old funeral
director in Ocala, Florida

I've often wondered what kind of funeral I want for myself. The only thing I know I want is confetti cannons to blow confetti all over the people who are there. As soon as the preacher says, "Amen," on the closing prayer, poof: confetti everywhere! I ask families what message they what conveyed, and I think for me, I want people to remember that I did my best to serve. I always did what I thought was right. I don't want it to be a sad affair. I think I'd like for my friends to speak. Those types of services, for me, are more meaningful. The minister, unless he's a really good friend, feels the need to keep everything solemn and dignified. That's okay for some people.

I want a funeral that's a "behind the scenes" funeral, meaning I don't want it to be what it's supposed to be. I want it to be fun and lighthearted. I want my music played; I don't want Amazing Grace just because it's supposed to be. I don't want the poem "The Dash" read at my funeral. I want my dash told by my friends and family. I've spent my life planning other people's funerals, asking questions until I find that one meaningful thing I can use to make the service an experience. I hope the funeral director who plans my funeral is like me.

*

BRIAN VAN HECK
Brian is a 41-year-old funeral director in
the Lake Norman area of North Carolina

My time spent as a funeral director has allowed me to think about my own mortality and how precious life is. I wish I could say that the only funerals I conduct are for 105-year-old men and women who have lived a full life, but that is not my reality. I have been able to reflect upon the type of service that I would like to have when my time on this earth comes to an end. My funeral will be very traditional in nature and reminiscent of the funeral masses of my youth when I served in the role of altar boy. Depending upon where I reside at the time of my death, I will have a time of visitation at the local funeral home. Then, my embalmed casketed body will be transported to my hometown of Grand Rapids, Michigan for a second period of visitation and funeral mass at the Catholic church that I grew up in, followed by interment at the Catholic cemetery where my family's plot is. While there will be some elements of personalization present at the informal visitations, the ceremony will be very traditional. The love of ritual and ceremony has been with me for many years and my wishes for my funeral have remained constant in a world that is ever-changing around me.

*

KIMBERLY VARELA
Kimberly is a 41-year-old funeral director
and embalmer in Westland, Michigan

I wanted to be cremated until I got into the industry. I have a very visceral reaction when I think about it now. A few years ago I decided on a green burial. As a Pagan, tree-hugging dirt worshiper, it seems most natural. I love the look of cemeteries but like the idea of being in a preserve where animals are in their native environment. I have no wish to leave any type of memorial to myself or have any type of preservation. I want to return back to the earth. When I think about it, there is a sense of calm.

*

DAN WELCH
Dan is a 30-year-old funeral director and
embalmer in Wichita, Kansas

My wife and I frequently discuss this because I am very adamant about my wishes for my funeral someday. At this point in my life I have made it well known that I want a simplistic, yet meaningful traditional service followed by ground burial in the family cemetery. I want to have a set visitation time when friends and family can pay their respects, as well as comfort one another and share memories about what a great guy I was.

For the service itself, I want to focus on my faith and my hobbies including hunting and my favorite sport team. It is important to me to give friends and family a time to share their memories. I want a procession to take place from the church to the cemetery, as I feel that is an important time for the community, though they may not know me, to honor my passing.

*

CHAPTER EIGHTEEN

Changing Trends

In any creative industry, the fact that others are moving in a certain direction is always proof positive, at least to me, that a new direction is the only direction. -GEORGE LOIS

Historically, funeral customs have largely been shaped by culture, geographical and economic influences. Over time those customs have fallen by the wayside. Personal wishes, environmental impact, and scattered family are but a few of the current influences. How have funerals changed in the past twenty years, and how do you think they will change over the next twenty years?

*

STEPHEN BARON
Stephen is a 64-year-old funeral service
licensee in Grand Haven, Michigan

As I see it, two events in the year 1963 served as a catalyst for the changes in how we do and have done funerals over the past twenty years, and for several years before that.

First off, the publishing and release of Jessica Mitford's book, *The American Way of Death*, caused many people to begin to question anything and everything related to death, and the practices and rituals surrounding death. Whether it was the answers gleaned from those questions or the lack of answers received, it is a widely held opinion that as a result of the book, the seeds of change brought about the highly individualized and more secular funeral and memorial service.

Also that year, the world witnessed firsthand via television the funeral of President John F. Kennedy. During that service the president's brother, Robert, spoke. Today it is very commonplace to have a eulogist or even several other participants, but to a nation in deep mourning in the mid-twentieth century, this was new and refreshing. It was very unusual to have anyone other than the clergy participate in that way. It added some of the first glimpses of individualism to funeral services. It was seen as something very personal coming to an event that formerly had been heavy with empty or misunderstood ritual for many.

As I look back at my career, these two events, along with our increased comfort with the absence of the deceased at their own funeral, and the ease with which we create great physical distance between our family members and friends, have caused us to change and weaken our traditions. It is hard to guess what changes could occur in the way we plan and execute funeral ceremonies in the future. With the advances in communication technology alone, I am sure there are changes ahead that we cannot imagine. I have to believe that our human need to gather together in the face of death and loss will somehow remain a driving force in the way we honor our dead.

*

CHASTIN BRINKLEY
Chastin is a 47-year-old funeral director, embalmer
and cremation specialist in Buckley, Washington

There has been a steady decline of funerals over the past twenty years with more people choosing cremation. In the past, when a family selected cremation, they opted not to have a memorial service. Now, we are starting to see more memorial services when cremation is selected. This year we have also had more witnessed cremations than in the past. A witness cremation is when the family watches the cremation container being placed into the cremation chamber. This is equivalent to watching a casket being lowered into the ground.

As funeral directors, we know the positive benefits from having meaningful funeral or memorial services, viewing, and accompanying the deceased throughout the burial or to watch them being placed into the cremation chamber. We also know how detrimental it can be to survivors when families do nothing after a death, or pretend every-thing is normal.

Since the beginning of time, when there was a death, there was a ceremony. Each generation has their own ideas on how the ceremony should be carried out. I do not know what the future holds for us. I only wish we could use history and past experiences to improve our ways to help those when death touches them.

263

*

JENNI BRYANT
Jenni is a 41-year-old funeral director
and embalmer in Maryville, Tennessee

I have been a funeral director for over sixteen years, and in that short time I have seen many changes! The cremation rate is quickly rising in my area. And families are spread out all over the place! Many will opt for cremation in order to have the service at a convenient time for everyone. So many people choose to wait until the weekend to have a service now because people can't take time off work.

Also, funerals have become more personalized. They are more about the person and telling the story of their life. There is not always a minister or preacher officiating the service anymore. Many family members choose to do the eulogy themselves or hire a certified celebrant. And not all families want to sit in the chapel of the funeral home and listen to sad music on the organ. We are having funerals outside, at our pavilion, with food and drink and good music. A true celebration of life!

*

JASON RYAN ENGLER
Jason is a 36-year-old funeral director, certified celebrant,
and cremation historian in Rogers, Arkansas

The drastic changes our profession has experienced in the last twenty years is mind-boggling. The focus of the funeral has gone from the generic to the personal. While some families still seem to choose "what dad had twenty years ago," many are opting for personalized celebrations of life that reflect their unique character.

In the history of funeral service, it was often discussed that a family should purchase a funeral that matched a person's station in life—and the funny thing is that this has not changed. Funeral and memorial services are more commonly reflecting the mindset and individuality of those who die. While the focus is less on products, it is becoming more focused on service. In the next two decades, I feel like we are going to see this evolution come to its ultimate realization as new generations make their wishes known, and as death becomes less about the process and more about the individual it is celebrating.

*

SHARON GEE-MASCARELLO
Sharon is a 53-year-old funeral director and embalming instructor
in the Mortuary Science Program at Wayne State University in Detroit

Maintaining relevance in the classroom after thirty years is challenging. Sharing examples of traditional three-day funerals is met with wonderment and puzzled expressions on my students' faces. I continue to insist that it is as unusual to hold a birthday party without the guest of honor or a wedding without the couple, as it is to have a funeral without the one who is dead being the main focal point. We go through, rather than around, rites of passage. I am death-accepting, and cherish rituals that honor this passage in the deceased's presence.

*

LOUISE GOHMANN
Louise is a 61-year-old mortuary school educator
and funeral director in Jeffersonville, Indiana

Funerals have changed considerably over the last twenty years. In the past they were traditional, almost cookie-cutter. You could pick out the top three hymns and likely be guaranteed you would hear them. Now, funerals are much more than that. They are celebrations, and events. Less "Rock of Ages" and more "I Want to Rock All Night!" Burial clothes are no longer stiff suits or dresses. Now it is not unusual to bury people in their comfiest clothes, or even pajamas. The trip to the grave is not just in a hearse, it is in the back of a pickup truck, fire truck, or motorcycle.

How will it change? Perhaps a movement back to visitations in the home. I don't believe that the change is a negative thing. Families are bringing children to the funeral homes again, and funerals have become as much a family reunion as anything else. Whatever gives a family comfort, and helps them remember their loved one.

*

KAREN JELLY
Karen is a 44-year-old funeral director
and mortician in Havre, Montana

Funerals have changed so much over the past twenty years. Twenty years ago, the Catholic church did not allow cremated remains in the church. Cremation was not the accepted norm, and no one would ever think of handling a memorial service on their own. Our do-it-yourself society has contributed to the direct cremation trend in our society, often with disastrous results. People who are planning a memorial service for the first time have no concept of the time and effort that goes into planning the service, arranging for all the music, the flowers, getting everything to the minister, and all the little details that funeral directors have been trained in. I don't even think about them anymore, I just handle them. And often, those who handle their own memorial service have little to no idea what is available for memorialization. We bring ideas to the arrangement that can really personalize services for families, whether burial or cremation. Sadly enough, there are many families who don't believe that having a memorial service or gathering is necessary to help with the healing process. It is my firm belief that having some type of gathering for those who knew the deceased will help their loved ones begin to heal.

More recently, I have seen families who are more involved in the planning of their service. They are more outspoken about the songs sung, or the casket or urn, or maybe just where they are sitting. I believe this is a very good trend, as they are taking back control in a situation that deprives them of a great deal of control.

In the next twenty years, I hope to see more people utilizing funeral directors' training and experience for memorial services, as I expect the cremation trend will continue to grow. Memorial services and funeral services are important. They remind us of what we believe in or what our core values are.

*

CORIANN MARTIN
Coriann is a 42-year-old funeral director
and embalmer in Kenosha, Wisconsin

Over the past twenty years, funerals have changed but I can't say they've changed as dramatically as you might think over that period of time. Traditions haven't so much changed as I mostly see new versions of those traditions emerging. Demographics play a big part in change. Cremation is increasing and I think it will continue to do so as people become more eco-conscious or fail to see the value in viewing the body. My biggest fear for change is when people avoid facing the reality of death and grieving because it's uncomfortable or too hard to deal with. I feel like this delays accepting the healing process.

*

LACY ROBINSON
Lacy is a 38-year-old Director of Member Development for the
National Funeral Directors Association in Brookfield, Wisconsin

Funeral events and mourning rituals have changed drastically in the last twenty-plus years. At one time every person who knew the deceased went to the visitation, funeral, committal service and after service meal. Now people pick the one event that works with their schedule and that's it. In regards to family members making decisions, funeral directors are seeing more and more families who want privacy or prefer to condense funeral events in a very short time period. They also have fewer ties to traditions. Funeral directors often ask themselves the question, "Do families value funeral service less?" I believe they do.

Dr. Alan Wolfelt, founder of Center for Loss and Life Transition, says, "Unfortunately, not understanding the why, or the value, of the elements, many grieving families forego them. Too often today they are stripping the funeral bare of ceremonial elements in favor of direct disposition. What they do not realize is that the more they chip away at the full ceremony, the more they run the risk of missing the sweet spot of a meaningful funeral experience."

Families have gone from having a two- to three-day event to planning an event without their loved one present which may even take place a month after the death has occurred. There are a variety of reasons why families are moving away from traditional funeral rituals, ranging from a disconnect from faith to wanting something that is convenient for everyone. This de-ritualization that has evolved among families has impacted funeral service and has certainly impacted how people mourn and heal following death of a loved one.

I am optimistic about the future of funeral service despite the many challenges that exist. I am starting to see classic funeral traditions slowly filter their way back into how families honor a person's life. I also meet funeral directors throughout the year who invest countless hours to communicating the value of funerals through valuable community outreach programs. These are the same funeral directors who are idea generators and appreciate the unique requests families may share during the arrangement conference.

*

SHAWNA RODABAUGH
Shawna is a 37-year-old funeral director and
embalmer in Mount Pleasant, Michigan

I think services have become far more personal and, for the most part, have moved away from traditional, religion-centered services, to services that are more about the deceased. This is when services are actually chosen. The trend toward cremation has left many without services at all, whether it is chosen because of a genuine desire not to have a service, or out of financial need. In the future, I see families starting to take the services more into their own hands, choosing for a burial or cremation that is immediate, then having gatherings with family and friends on their own.

*

STEVE TWEEDLE
Steve is a 42-year-old funeral
director in Ocala, Florida

I've seen a lot of changes. Cremation has become more prevalent, services are abbreviated, and there are more evolved memorial products. I think as long as funeral directors continue to evolve their thinking, it's all positive change.

I know some funeral director friends who have a high burial percentage, seventy to eighty percent. We are at seventy percent cremation. I tell them it's coming, and they better start changing to accommodate it. I tell them to start now and educate the public that just because people are choosing cremation doesn't mean they are limiting themselves to no service. We have been active in trying to educate the public and it amazes me when I say to a family, "Did you know you can still have the body present for a service even though you chose cremation?" and they didn't know.

*

BRIAN VAN HECK
Brian is a 41-year-old funeral director in
the Lake Norman area of North Carolina

The world we live in today seems to be changing at an incredibly rapid pace, yet the need for tending to the dead has been around since the beginning of time. At least in our North American culture, we have come to expect instantaneous results in just about every arena of life and we become aggravated if we have to wait a few extra seconds for a website to load or our fast food to be prepared. This fast food mentality has even found its way into my profession as a funeral director. The biggest change that has occurred in funeral service in the last twenty years is the increased number of families selecting cremation as the method of final disposition for their loved one and I believe this number will continue to rise. Additionally, more and more people will plan their own services because they are not aware of what a funeral director does. We have become such a do-it-yourself society, even pushing away help from professionals at a time of such great need in our lives, when our loved ones have died.

*

As men, we are all equal
in the presence of death.

PUBLILIUS SYRUS

*

CHAPTER NINETEEN

what we want you to know

We are at our very best, and we are happiest, when we are fully engaged in work we enjoy on the journey toward the goal we've established for ourselves. -EARL NIGHTINGALE

Although the funeral industry is built around death, it is surprisingly full of life. A calling to comfort the bereaved, tend to the dead, and taking time from their own families to ensure that our final farewell is memorable, the funeral industry is humanity at its finest. What do you want people to know about being a funeral director?

*

STEPHEN BARON
Stephen is a 64-year-old funeral service
licensee in Grand Haven, Michigan

My father told me many years before I selected funeral service as my life's work, "If you decide to make this your life's work, be aware that it is never an easy task. You will see and experience great sadness many times over. Hopefully you will walk with friends and with strangers alike during the worst moments of their lives and by doing so, you will help them all in some small way to move forward from their loss." Our world needs more caregivers. It is truly the most rewarding work I can imagine and I am proud and humbled to be a part of this profession.

*

CHASTIN BRINKLEY
Chastin is a 47-year-old funeral director, embalmer
and cremation specialist in Buckley, Washington

Being a funeral director is hard work. We have long hours and sleepless nights. We work holidays. We work with hazardous chemicals and infectious people. Our business is not taxpayer subsidized but it is burdened with government regulations. So why did we choose this profession? Most of us have a true desire to help people. Some say it is a calling, but I have never heard my name. Who doesn't have empathy or want to help when you see someone hurting? I believe God has given each of us special gifts to help people. Mine is being a funeral director and embalmer.

*

JENNI BRYANT
Jenni is a 41-year-old funeral director
and embalmer in Maryville, Tennessee

I want people to know that being a funeral director is a true calling. I love helping people, listening to their stories and helping them plan a meaningful celebration of life. Some days are harder than others. We miss first steps, birthday parties, family gatherings, baseball games, Thanksgiving dinner, and Christmas morning. But it's

274

okay. It is a calling. It's what I do. And I wouldn't have it any other way. These things make me appreciate the time I do get to spend with my family and friends that much more!

*

JASON RYAN ENGLER
Jason is a 36-year-old funeral director, certified celebrant,
and cremation historian in Rogers, Arkansas

We are human. We feel, we see, we experience, we love. We are not typically the lugubrious ghouls that one considers when one thinks of funeral directors—though we all have our moments. We are community individuals that care about members of society and what it means to lose a person to death. We truly care for people, or we wouldn't be where we are in our professions. Most of us have felt loss on some level, so we know what it means to celebrate life each day. In the face of death we can stand beside you and guide you through the entire process. We are always here when you need us.

*

SHARON GEE-MASCARELLO
Sharon is a 53-year-old funeral director and embalming instructor
in the Mortuary Science Program at Wayne State University in Detroit

My students say it best: "I want to help people." Amen.

*

LOUISE GOHMANN
Louise is a 61-year-old mortuary school educator
and funeral director in Jeffersonville, Indiana

To quote an old army slogan, the funeral business is "the toughest

275

job you'll ever love." That being said, when it becomes just a job, it's time to get out. I love this business with its ups and downs, frustrations and triumphs. If you're becoming a funeral director to get rich, you'd better rethink your career path. It is a round-the-clock job every day of the year. We never close. If you want to be a funeral director because you have a sincere desire to help people and make a difference in the lives of grieving people, then be welcome.

*

KAREN JELLY
Karen is a 44-year-old funeral director
and mortician in Havre, Montana

Being a funeral director is the most wonderful and most exhausting career there is. We are able to come into a family's life at the worst possible moment and provide guidance and comfort to that family. However, we are also sleep deprived, exhausted, overworked, and, for those of us working in small town funeral homes, we have no real personal life to speak of. Most people go home at a set time every day or night and spend time with their friends and family.

We are on call, often seven days a week, fifty-two weeks a year. When the phone rings, we answer it. When someone has passed, we go, even if we are in the middle of dinner or at church. We often embalm all night and meet with families during the day, trying to stifle the yawns, not because we are bored, but because we have had no rest. Very seldom do we get a whole weekend off, and when we do, we make the most of it.

Please understand, I love what I do. My client families are almost as important to me as my husband and children. I strive to provide the service they want to memorialize their loved one. And often, I knew and cared for their loved one, and am grieving with them, although they don't know it.

So, if a funeral director has tried but is unable to provide what you want, please don't be too harsh. He or she is probably exhausted. The one thing to keep in mind is that we are people too, and everyone has a bad day occasionally.

*

CORIANN MARTIN
Coriann is a 42-year-old funeral director
and embalmer in Kenosha, Wisconsin

Being a funeral director isn't a job, it's a calling. It's a career that you can't turn off when you go home. It's who you are and if you don't have it in you to put your heart into everything you do, it remains just a job. As in any profession, you find people who lose their passion or lose sight of the privilege they've been given. I believe that those who recognize how blessed they are to have the gift of helping people through the worst days of their lives will always know a unique kind of joy that others will never know.

*

LACY ROBINSON
Lacy is a 38-year-old Director of Member Development for the
National Funeral Directors Association in Brookfield, Wisconsin

The older I get, the more grateful I am for the experiences I have had in funeral service. Through this profession I've grown mentally and emotionally. Looking back on the funeral homes I've worked for, the funeral directors I've had the opportunity to meet on my travels and the passionate people working hard to provide quality products, I know this is exactly where I need to be professionally.

*

SHAWNA RODABAUGH
Shawna is a 37-year-old funeral director and
embalmer in Mount Pleasant, Michigan

Every funeral director is in this field out of love. In order for us to do what we do every day, we have to have an intense love of the work, and love for the families.

*

STEVE TWEEDLE
Steve is a 42-year-old funeral
director in Ocala, Florida

This job is not easy. We are not all rich. A VAST majority of us work very hard and the amount of personal sacrifice is staggering. We give up our family to be there with yours. We suffer with loss as much as you suffer. I've buried the preacher that was at the church I was raised in, I did the services for my elementary school principal. We all take the job home with us. I can't tell you how many times I've woken up in the middle of the night suddenly wondering if I've ordered a casket or the right flowers. My kids know the funeral home inside and out. They spend two to three hours there per day waiting for me to finish my day. They sacrifice too. We get up at 3 a.m. in the morning to be with your family, and are back up and to work at 8 a.m. to be with your neighbor's family. We are volunteers at nursing homes, churches, civic groups, and public events. We have a vast network of friends and family who will do whatever they can to help. I can call my sister if I need to and ask for something for a family for a funeral and she will stop what she's doing, and you don't even know her. I can call a friend of mine and have a horse at your funeral if you want, or I can have a band that plays rock music. Most importantly, I want people to know that we care deeply about what we do.

*

BRIAN VAN HECK
Brian is a 41-year-old funeral director in
the Lake Norman area of North Carolina

Despite the stories about funeral directors who make the evening news, *60 Minutes, Dateline NBC* or some other form of media, funeral directors are caring individuals who want nothing more than to walk with families and honor the life of their deceased loved one. I have learned a great deal about myself and human nature along my life's path and especially in my time, thus far, as a funeral director. Every life matters and every life deserves to have a proper and honoring ceremony to commemorate the life of the person who has died. I am blessed to be able to walk with the bereaved, gently guiding them on the path of life and living, as together we create a funeral. I have picked up and been given many articles, books, cartoons, and so on, about my profession over the years but the one that summarizes what I do best reads as follows.

HE NEVER TURNS AWAY
Unknown

They come to him for help when they need it the most.
Some numbed by their loss, some shattered, they say:
"This is someone we loved. We entrust him to you."

And even when he's faced with the crumpled innocence of the youngest
asking, "Why?"

And he has to find the childlike words to answer a question that even
theologians struggle with, he never turns away.

He gives them the consolation of tradition.

He shows them how to accept their tragedy
with grace.

He helps them cope with their grief.

He guides them back to the active world of the living.

He is a funeral director.

He practices the most emotionally demanding and least understood of all
professions.

He faces up to traumas every day that most people only have to deal
with once or twice in a lifetime.

He has earned the deepest thanks from anyone who
ever leaned on his compassion for support,
who turned to him and found that
he would never turn away.

*

*

KIMBERLY VARELA
Kimberly is a 41-year-old funeral director
and embalmer in Westland, Michigan

We are not strange or weird. We are normal people who have families, chores, bills, and emotions like anyone else. We can laugh, and often do. We suffer loss and bury or cremate our own family. We have to be stoic and strong for our families but sometimes we go in the back and have a small panic attack because we don't yet know how to meet a family's request for their loved one.

We often don't take good enough care of ourselves and question if we are the right person for this job. We spend days in complete silence because those we serve don't speak to us in words. We shed a tear when we hear Taps, or the voice of a child who asks if Daddy is ever coming back.

We miss out on a lot because of the time and dedication we put into our work, and the odd hours that we are called upon. We are not necessarily fascinated by death but we can stand comfortably close to it on a daily basis. We often appreciate things more because we have files of examples of when it can all be taken away.

We don't walk a fine line and we try not to spend too much time on one side or the other because we don't want to lose our own humanity. We are not reapers or revenants. We are caretakers. We serve those who can never thank us.

*

DAN WELCH
Dan is a 30-year-old funeral director and
embalmer in Wichita, Kansas

Being a funeral director is one of the most challenging yet rewarding jobs available. I have oftentimes joked with colleagues and friends that everyone would be a funeral director if it were an eight-to-five job because you really do get to experience things that most people don't have the opportunity to. I think it is also important for people to know that funeral directors are people too. We are not robot order takers. We do care about the needs, desires, and wants of each family who walks through our door. Our goal is to help families recover from their loss in a healthy manner. We are not scary people. We do not like to play with dead bodies. We are moms, dads, brothers, sisters, and friends—just like anyone else.

*

CHAPTER TWENTY

Meet the writers

A good story invites us into someone else's world
where we learn, discover commonalities, and
leave with compassion and understanding.

LYNDA CHELDELIN FELL

*

*

STEPHEN BARON
Stephen is a 64-year-old funeral service
licensee in Grand Haven, Michigan

Stephen W. Baron is a second generation funeral director. He attended Grand Rapids Community College, Grand Valley State University, and received his mortuary science degree from The Indiana College of Mortuary Science in Indianapolis. After having spent many years with Metcalf & Jonkhoff Funeral Service, Inc. in Grand Rapids, and one of its predecessor firms, Jonkhoff Funeral  Homes, Inc. of Grand Rapids and Caledonia, Steve retired in 2011. Upon retirement, he became Director of Memorial Ministries for Westminster Church in Grand Rapids. He works with parishioners and their funeral directors in the planning of funeral and memorial services, and assists church members and friends of the congregation in pre-planning service content. Steve is an advocate of strong clergy-funeral director working relationships and has worked with students of both professions to help strengthen those ties.

Steve and his wife Cindy reside in Grand Haven, Michigan. They have four grown children and eleven grandchildren. They enjoy both foreign and domestic travel, history, and music of all kinds.

*

CHASTIN BRINKLEY
Chastin is a 47-year-old funeral director, embalmer
and cremation specialist in Buckley, Washington
www.weeksfuneralhomes.com

Chastin Brinkley was born in Amarillo, Texas, and graduated from Dallas Institute of Funeral Service in 1991, with an Associate of Applied Science Degree. He served his apprenticeship at Restland Funeral Home, one of the largest funeral home and cemetery combinations in Dallas, Texas. After licensure, Chastin worked for Schooler-Gordon-Blackburn-Shaw Funeral Directors in his hometown. He then moved to Enumclaw, Washington, and has worked for the past nineteen years with the Weeks' family of funeral homes. In 2016, Chastin completed over 130 contact hours of Advanced and Advanced II Post Mortem Reconstructive Surgery instruction at the prestigious Fountain National Academy in Springfield, Missouri. He is a member of both the National Funeral Directors Association and Washington State Funeral Directors Association.

*

JENNI BRYANT
Jenni is a 41-year-old funeral director
and embalmer in Maryville, Tennessee

Jenni Bryant was born and raised in Knoxville, Tennessee. She earned her Mortuary Science degree at Gupton-Jones College in Atlanta in 2000, and is a sixteen-year veteran of funeral service helping the families of Blount County, Tennessee, create memorable life celebration events.

Jenni is a licensed funeral director and embalmer with Smith Funeral & Cremation Service. She is a certified member of the Academy of Professional Funeral Service Practice and a member of the Tennessee Funeral Directors Association. In recent years Jenni has served on the Professional Development Committee for the National Funeral Directors Association, attended Meet the Mentors in 2012, and assisted Smith Funeral & Cremation Service in achieving NFDA's prestigious Pursuit of Excellence Best of the Best Award in 2014. As an active member of the community, Jenni serves as a school liaison, helps with the local career fairs, and devotes countless hours to the Variety's Katerpillar Kids Bereavement Camp in Knoxville, Tennessee.

*

LAUREN BUDROW
Lauren is a 44-year-old funeral director
and funeral service educator

Lauren Budrow was born in Indianapolis, Indiana. She was inspired by her father-in-law to pursue funeral service and earned her mortuary science degree from Vincennes University in 2002. While in school, Lauren worked part-time at a funeral home where she then completed her internship and worked full-time for eight years meeting families and directing funerals. In 2007, Lauren pursued her Master's in Business Administration from Butler University which she completed in 2012.

Since 2011, Lauren has been involved in funeral service education, teaching students and sharing stories to help prepare future funeral directors for the ups and downs of the demanding yet rewarding career in the funeral profession.

*

JASON RYAN ENGLER
Jason is a 36-year-old funeral director, certified celebrant,
and cremation historian in Rogers, Arkansas

Jason Ryan Engler is a licensed funeral director, cremation specialist, consultant and historian. He is an Insight Institute Certified Celebrant, a CANA certified crematory operator, and an ICCFA certified cremation arranger.

Jason speaks at conventions and meetings both locally and across the country, and is a frequent contributor to funeral and cremation trade journals. He is the official historian for the Cremation Association of North America, senior cremation advisor for the National Museum of Funeral History in Houston, officer and board member of the Arkansas Funeral Directors Association and the Northwest Arkansas Funeral Directors Association, and advisory board member of the Arkansas State University Mountain Home's Funeral Science Program. Jason resides in northwest Arkansas along with his miniature dachshund, Otto.

*

SHARON GEE-MASCARELLO
Sharon is a 53-year-old funeral director and embalming instructor
in the Mortuary Science Program at Wayne State University in Detroit

Sharon L. Gee-Mascarello is clinical faculty in the Eugene Applebaum College of Pharmacy and Health Sciences, Fundamental and Applied Sciences, Mortuary Science Program at Wayne State University in Detroit. She is the instructor of Embalming, Practicum Coordinator and teaches Comparative Religion and Presentation & Cosmetics. She is a member of the National Funeral Directors Association, Academy of Funeral Service Practice, Michigan Funeral Directors Association, Ohio Embalmer Association, Michigan Embalmers Society, American Society of Embalmers and British Institute of Embalmers, and is a

contributor to the textbook *Embalming: History, Theory, and Practice* by Robert G. Mayer. Sharon enjoys public speaking and writing articles on embalming-related topics. She is always eager to promote funeral service dialogues especially those concerning embalming, organ/tissue/eye donation, ethical decedent care and humanitarian service to client families. Sharon has been named Educator of the Year by Wayne State University, Mortuary Educator of the Year by the 100 Black Women of Funeral Service, and received Gift of Life Michigan's first ever Champion Award for opening dialogues among professionals that save and enhance lives through donation.

*

LOUISE GOHMANN
Louise is a 61-year-old mortuary school educator
and funeral director in Jeffersonville, Indiana

Louise "Lee" Gohmann is from New Albany, Indiana. She is a licensed funeral director and embalmer in Indiana and Florida, and instructs the anatomy and funeral service social sciences at Mid-America College of Funeral Service. Since joining Mid-America College of Funeral Service, Lee has discovered the joy in training  tomorrow's funeral directors today. She feels that continuing her work as a funeral director while teaching gives her a special closeness to her students. She is fond of saying "I walk where you walk."

*

KAREN JELLY
Karen is a 44-year-old funeral director
and mortician in Havre, Montana

Karen Jelly was born in Des Moines, Iowa. She graduated from Noxon High School in Noxon, Montana, and went earned a business degree from Sheridan College in Wyoming. Karen obtained her mortuary science degree from Arapahoe Community College in Littleton, Colorado, graduating in 2012. She became fully licensed as a funeral director in the state of Montana in 2013.

*

CODY JONES

Cody is a 37-year-old progressive funeral home owner
and funeral director in Bryan-College Station, Texas
Callaway-Jones Funeral and Cremation Centers
CallawayJones.com | cjones@callawayjones.com

Cody D. Jones is a native Texan and fifth-generation funeral director who assumed managing responsibility for Callaway-Jones Funeral Center and Crematories in 2004. Cody is also the founder of Pet Legacies Cremation Services. He graduated from Bryan High School, Southern Methodist University, and Commonwealth Funeral Institute of Houston. Awards and honors include the National Funeral Service Honor Society, and Harvard University's Meet the Mentors Funeral Program. Cody is past president of the Southeast Texas Funeral Directors Association, and is past board member of the Texas Funeral Directors Association where he served on both the Legislative and Membership Committees. As a respected community leader in Bryan-College Station, Cody has been honored by the Bryan Rotary Club as a Paul Harris Fellow and the Bryan-College Station Chamber of Commerce's Leadership Brazos Program. A competitive soccer player, Cody competed on the Olympic Development team in Europe, and still plays locally. Cody and his wife, Chelsea, enjoy Aggie sports events and golf and skiing on their travels.

*
CORIANN MARTIN
Coriann is a 42-year-old funeral director
and embalmer in Kenosha, Wisconsin
Piasecki-Althaus Funeral Home
www.piasecki-althaus.com | pnb4me@wi.rr.com

Coriann Martin was born and raised in Milwaukee, Wisconsin. She started her career in a large Milwaukee funeral home where she received hands-on training for eight months before enrolling in the Mortuary Science program at the MATC-West Allis Campus in 1995. She apprenticed in funeral homes in the Milwaukee and Waukesha areas, and completed her education and passed her state boards in 1997.

Coriann moved to the Appleton area in 1998, and spent the next three years and gained invaluable experience working for a progressive six-hundred-plus call volume funeral home with five locations.

Returning closer to home in 2001, she has been with Piasecki-Althaus Funeral Home in Kenosha ever since. Coriann expanded her talents by acquiring her insurance license and Illinois funeral director license.

*

JENNIFER PARKS
Jennifer is a 45-year-old certified funeral
celebrant in Santa Barbara, California

Moving to Santa Barbara in 2002, Jennifer found an unlikely home at McDermott-Crockett Mortuary. Under the tutelage of Richard Crockett, she learned all facets of mortuary management and funeral arrangements and became general manager upon his retirement in 2010. From working with families at the beginning of a life as a doula to assisting families at the end, Jennifer was drawn to the importance of honoring each person's love story for those who have passed and the loved ones left behind. By truly listening to families in grief, she has the unique opportunity to suggest and incorporate healing rituals, encourage participation and honestly pause in a time of care and reflection just as our ancestors did hundreds of years ago. Her compassionate and empathetic nature lends itself to her profession to truly help those in pain, honor their relationships, and act as a guide in the first steps on the journey through grief and loss.

She and her husband Todd have been happily married for twenty-five years and have three amazing kids. Her parents, her sister (her rock and best friend in the world), as well as a bevy of friends who have become family, round out her reason for being.

*
LACY ROBINSON
Lacy is a 38-year-old Director of Member Development for the
National Funeral Directors Association in Brookfield, Wisconsin
www.NFDA.org

Lacy Robinson is Director of Member
Development for the National Funeral
Directors Association. She develops
and facilitates training programs for
NFDA members, and presents
continuing education programs at
local, state, and national levels,
establishing NFDA as the leading
provider of training and development
for funeral professionals. Prior to
NFDA, Lacy served as Director of

Professional Development for Aurora Casket Company. Lacy is a
licensed funeral director/embalmer, a certified funeral celebrant, and
certified member of the Academy of Professional Funeral Service
Practice. She graduated from Georgetown College with a Bachelor's
in Communications. She is also a graduate of Mid-America College of
Funeral Service.

As an active member of the Bluegrass Toastmasters Group, Lacy has
achieved the designation Competent Communicator. Lacy also serves
on the Board of Trustees for the Academy of Professional Funeral
Service Practice and is vice-chairperson of the Mid-America College
of Funeral Service Advisory Board.

*

SHAWNA RODABAUGH
Shawna is a 37-year-old funeral director and
embalmer in Mount Pleasant, Michigan

Shawna Rodabaugh is from central Michigan, and earned her mortuary science education at Wayne State University in Detroit in 2003. She spent ten years as a funeral director and embalmer in both Michigan and Florida before moving into the educational field of death care. She currently serves as the manager of anatomical laboratories at Central Michigan University where she cares  and advocates for the anatomical donors who serve in the medical educational capacity after death.

*

STEVE TWEEDLE
Steve is a 42-year-old funeral
director in Ocala, Florida

Steve Tweedle was born in Miami and
moved to Belleview, Florida, at age five.
He earned an Associate degree in
Funeral Services at St. Petersburg
College and went to work for the funeral
home in the small town he grew up in.
He still resides in that town, and has
worked for the same company for
twenty-five years.

*

BRIAN VAN HECK
Brian is a 41-year-old funeral director in
the Lake Norman area of North Carolina

Brian M. Van Heck is a native of
Grand Rapids, Michigan, and
currently lives in the Lake Norman
area of North Carolina with his wife,
Elizabeth. Besides completing his
mortuary science education at
Gupton-Jones College of Funeral
Service in Atlanta, Brian is a graduate
of St. John's University in Minnesota
where he earned a Bachelor's degree
in theology. He furthered his education by receiving a Master's in
counseling from Michigan State University.

Brian possesses nearly twenty years of unique funeral service
experience. His personal philosophy for serving families in their time
of need is to walk with them to create a meaningful and unique
ceremony that honors the life of their loved one. Serving community
through funeral service is paramount to Brian; he considers it not only
a ministry, but also his life's calling. In addition to serving families,
Brian is an active volunteer in community outreach programs that
promote recovery and personal growth. Brian and Elizabeth enjoy
spending time together outdoors and especially on the water where
Brian is a competitive slalom skier.

*

KIMBERLY VARELA
Kimberly is a 41-year-old funeral director
and embalmer in Westland, Michigan
Husband Family Funeral Home | RHusband.com

Kimberly is a graduate of the Wayne State University Mortuary Science program where she was awarded the 2012 Gerald P. Cavalier Excellence in Embalming Award. Her unique experience as the child of career-enlisted military parents gives her insight into the importance of dignity, respect, and honor when it comes to service.

As a hospice volunteer, Kimberly has well-rounded experience helping families in time of grief. She enjoys gardening, spending time with family and friends, and playing with her three rescue pets. She currently works as funeral director and embalmer for Husband Family Funeral Home in Westland, Michigan.

*

DAN WELCH
Dan is a 30-year-old funeral director
and embalmer in Wichita, Kansas
welch.dan@hotmail.com

Dan was born and raised in Manhattan, Kansas, and began his studies at Central Bible College in Springfield, Missouri, where he earned a Bachelor's degree in Pastoral Ministries. In 2008, Dan accepted a position as an associate pastor in Wichita, Kansas. Throughout his time on staff at the church, Dan felt as though he was being led into a different facet of ministry. In 2009, Dan began working on an as-needed basis at a local funeral home. He quickly realized that funeral service was the facet of ministry he desired to be in, and he began studying at the Dallas Institute of Funeral Service. While attending school, Dan worked for one of the largest embalming services in the country where he furthered his skills as an embalmer and restorative artist. He currently resides in Wichita, with his wife, Kateland, and their young daughter. Dan is a licensed funeral director and embalmer and is recognized as a certified crematory operator. He is actively involved in both the Kansas Funeral Directors Association and the National Funeral Directors Association.

One smile can change a mood.
One hello can change a day.
One story can change a life.

LYNDA CHELDELIN FELL

*

FROM LYNDA CHELDELIN FELL

THANK YOU

I am deeply indebted to the writers of *Through the Eyes of a Funeral Director.* Such a collaboration sheds insight into an industry filled with the most compassionate people in the world. In addition to demanding schedules, unpredictable moments, and supporting the bereaved in their darkest hour, each one carved out time to pen their answers for this book. No small task! A big thank you to Brian Van Heck for collaborating on this project and helping bring it to fruition. What a wonderful way to help readers better understand such an honorable line of work.

It's been said that pictures alone without the written word leaves half the story untold. A good story intrigues and invites us to go beyond the edge of our own life into the world of another where we discover, learn, find commonality, and—perhaps most important—we leave with deeper understanding of one another. That's what this book is all about.

Lynda Cheldelin Fell

She who heals others heals herself.

LYNDA CHELDELIN FELL

*

LYNDA CHELDELIN FELL

Considered a pioneer in the field of inspirational hope, Lynda Cheldelin Fell has a passion for storytelling and producing groundbreaking projects that create a legacy of help, healing, and hope.

She is co-founder of the International Grief Institute, CEO of AlyBlue Media, and an international bestselling author and creator of the award-winning book series Grief Diaries, Real Life Diaries, and Career Diaries. Her repertoire of interviews include Dr. Martin Luther King's daughter, Trayvon Martin's mother, sisters of the late Nicole Brown Simpson, Pastor Todd Burpo of Heaven Is For Real, CNN commentator Dr. Ken Druck, and other societal newsmakers on finding healing and hope in the aftermath of life's harshest challenges.

Lynda's own story began in 2007, when she had an alarming dream about her young teenage daughter, Aly. In the dream, Aly was a backseat passenger in a car that veered off the road and landed in a lake. Aly sank with the car, leaving behind an open book floating face down on the water. Two years later, Lynda's dream became reality when her daughter was killed as a backseat passenger in a car accident while coming home from a swim meet. Overcome with grief, Lynda's forty-six-year-old husband suffered a major stroke that left him with severe disabilities, changing the family dynamics once again.

The following year, Lynda was invited to share her remarkable story about finding hope after loss, and she accepted. That cathartic experience inspired her to create groundbreaking projects spanning national events, radio, film and books to help others who share the same journey feel less alone. Now a dedicated story curator, educator, and speaker, Lynda is passionate about harnessing the power of storytelling to help raise awareness and foster understanding about the complexities of life.

lynda@lyndafell.com | www.lyndafell.com

ALYBLUE MEDIA TITLES

Real Life Diaries: Through the Eyes of a Funeral Director
Real Life Diaries: Living with a Brain Injury
Real Life Diaries: Through the Eyes of DID
Real Life Diaries: Through the Eyes of an Eating Disorder
Real Life Diaries: Living with Endometriosis
Real Life Diaries: Living with Mental Illness
Grief Diaries: Victim Impact Statement
Grief Diaries: Hit by Impaired Driver
Grief Diaries: Surviving Loss of a Spouse
Grief Diaries: Surviving Loss of a Child
Grief Diaries: Surviving Loss of a Sibling
Grief Diaries: Surviving Loss of a Parent
Grief Diaries: Surviving Loss of an Infant
Grief Diaries: Surviving Loss of a Loved One
Grief Diaries: Surviving Loss by Suicide
Grief Diaries: Surviving Loss of Health
Grief Diaries: How to Help the Newly Bereaved
Grief Diaries: Loss by Impaired Driving
Grief Diaries: Loss by Homicide
Grief Diaries: Loss of a Pregnancy
Grief Diaries: Hello from Heaven
Grief Diaries: Grieving for the Living
Grief Diaries: Shattered
Grief Diaries: Project Cold Case
Grief Diaries: Poetry & Prose and More
Grief Diaries: Through the Eyes of Men
Grief Diaries: Will We Survive?
Grammy Visits From Heaven
Grandpa Visits From Heaven
Faith, Grief & Pass the Chocolate Pudding
Heaven Talks to Children
Color My Soul Whole
A Child is Missing: A True Story
A Child is Missing: Searching for Justice
Grief Reiki

Humanity's legacy of stories and storytelling
is the most precious we have.

DORIS LESSING

*

To share your story, visit
www.griefdiaries.com
www.RealLifeDiaries.com

PUBLISHED BY ALYBLUE MEDIA
Inside every human is a story worth sharing.
www.AlyBlueMedia.com

CPSIA information can be obtained
at www.ICGtesting.com
Printed in the USA
LVHW111000300520
657006LV00004B/1189

9 781944 328436